CHRISTMAS RECIPES FROM THE LION HOUSE

CHRISTMAS RECIPES FROM THE LION HOUSE

COMPILED BY
GLORIA W. RYTTING

Photographs by
Ramon Winegar

Deseret Book Company
Salt Lake City, Utah

Library of Congress Cataloging-in-Publication Data

Christmas recipes from the Lion House / compiled by Gloria W. Rytting.

    p. cm.
    Includes index.
    ISBN 0-87579-255-3
    1. Christmas cookery. 2. Lion House (Restaurant) I. Rytting, Gloria W.
TX739.2.C45C468   1989
641.5'66—dc20   89-35572
                                                  CIP

Printed in the United States of America

10   9   8   7   6   5   4   3   2

CONTENTS

PREFACE

Christmas, like no other time of the year, evokes our most cherished and delicious memories: tempting cranberry pies, fragrant fruitcakes, succulent roast turkey, and mouth-watering candies and confections. Christmas in 1859 at the Lion House, home of Mormon pioneer and prophet Brigham Young and his family, was just as memorable, with a grand holiday dinner for nearly seventy-five persons living in the house, including President Young, several of his wives, and forty children under the age of thirteen.

Today the Lion House is still special at Christmastime. While the Young family no longer resides there, the house bustles with guests attending banquets and luncheons, wedding receptions and birthday parties. Several hundred patrons lunch every weekday in the Pantry on the ground floor. Aromas of delectable home-cooked foods still waft the air, and the house is decorated in much the same manner as an old-fashioned Lion House Christmas, festooned with green garlands and red velvet ribbon and decorations.

These Christmas recipes from the Lion House will translate remembrances of Christmases past into the era of Christmas present—and in so doing, perhaps create some brand-new memories. We've included only our best holiday recipes, those that will adapt to a variety of needs and occasions. And they come not only from the files of the Lion House, but also from the kitchens of the good cooks and staff.

To begin your Yuletide cooking, you might invite family and friends to share the warmth of soup and breads. For holiday dinners, you can choose from traditional favorites, with all their trimmings, as well as change-of-pace feasts. Included are recipes that are on the lighter side for those who want low-fat or low-sugar choices.

Christmas is the season for sharing, and what more thoughtful way to say "Merry Christmas" than with a gaily wrapped gift from your own kitchen. Included are many of our favorites: pickles and jellies, spreads and sauces, special sweets, and suggestions for packaging.

Whatever your plans for celebrating the holidays, this book will give you not old-fashioned recipes, but perhaps some brand new ideas to help make the joys of the season—the good food, the good fellowship—thrive in your home. It's our merry Christmas present to you.

ACKNOWLEDGMENTS

We are grateful to the food specialists, cooks, bakers, housekeepers, hostesses, cashiers, waitresses, and office staff who serve at the Lion House. Many of the recipes in this collection are from these individuals. Without the special care and pride shown by all who work at the Lion House, this book would not have been possible.

oh what fun and noise!

REFRESHING
BEVERAGES AND
APPETIZERS

LION HOUSE WASSAIL

2¼ cups sugar
4 cups water
2 cinnamon sticks
8 allspice berries
10 cloves
1 piece ginger
4 cups orange juice
2 cups lemon juice
2 quarts apple cider or juice

Combine sugar and water. Boil 5 minutes. Remove from heat and add cinnamon sticks, allspice berries, cloves, and ginger. Cover and let stand in warm place for 1 hour. Strain. Just before serving, add juices and cider and bring quickly to boil. Remove from heat and serve. Makes 36 half-cup servings.

MULLED CRANBERRY DRINK

1 12-ounce package fresh cranberries
8 cups (2 quarts) water
1½ cups sugar
2 tablespoons grated orange peel
6 cinnamon sticks
12 whole cloves
4 cups orange juice
1 cup lemon juice
Thin lemon slices

Combine cranberries, water, sugar, orange peel, cinnamon sticks, and cloves in large pan and cook till cranberries are soft, about 15 minutes. Strain. Add juices. Do not boil but keep warm till ready to serve. Float thin lemon slice in each cup. Makes 24 half-cup servings.

HOLIDAY NOG

¼ *cup sugar*
½ *teaspoon cinnamon*
¼ *teaspoon ginger*
6 *eggs*
4 *cups orange juice*
4 *cups pineapple juice*
4 *cups ginger ale*
1 *pint orange sherbet*

Mix sugar, cinnamon, and ginger. Add eggs and beat well. Stir in juices. Chill. Just before serving, add ginger ale. Pour into punch bowl and add scoops of sherbet. Makes about 24 half-cup servings.

FIESTA CRUSH

4 *cups sugar*
6 *cups water*
5 *ripe bananas, peeled and mashed*
2½ *cups orange juice*
4 *cups pineapple juice*
½ *cup lemon juice*
2 12-*ounce cans carbonated lemon-*
   lime beverage

Combine sugar and water in saucepan and heat till sugar is dissolved. Cool. Mash bananas and combine with orange juice, pineapple juice, lemon juice, and sugar syrup. Pour into shallow pan and freeze. When ready to serve, remove from freezer to thaw slightly. Break into chunks and fill cups two-thirds full. Pour carbonated lemon-lime beverage over slush. Garnish each serving with a maraschino cherry or sprig of holly. Makes 25 half-cup servings.

ST. NICK'S LIME FIZZ

½ cup fresh lime juice
½ cup sugar
1½ cups pineapple juice
1 quart lime sherbet
1 16-ounce bottle carbonated lemon-
*   lime beverage*
Maraschino cherries
Thin slices of lime

Place lime juice, sugar, and pineapple juice in blender and whirl for 30 seconds. Add half the lime sherbet and whirl again for a few seconds. Pour into 8 10-ounce glasses (two-thirds full) and fill almost to top with carbonated lemon-lime beverage. Top each cup with a scoop of sherbet. Garnish with maraschino cherry and half slice of fresh lime. Serve with straw. Makes 8 servings.

GRAPE SPARKLE

2 cups sugar
4 cups water
2 cups grape juice
2 cups orange juice
½ cup lemon juice
1 12-ounce can carbonated gingerale
*   beverage*

Combine sugar and water in saucepan and heat till dissolved. Cool. Add grape juice, orange juice, and lemon juice. Pour into shallow pan and freeze. When ready to serve, remove from freezer and thaw slightly. Break up into chunks and fill punch cups two-thirds full. Pour gingerale over slush and serve. Makes 20 half-cup servings.

HOLLY BERRY SLUSH

2 cups sugar
3½ cups water
1 10-ounce package frozen raspberries
l cup orange juice
1 20-ounce can crushed pineapple,
  undrained
¼ cup lemon juice
Red food coloring (optional)
2 12-ounce cans carbonated lemon-
  lime beverage

Combine sugar and water in saucepan and heat till sugar is dissolved. Remove from heat and stir in frozen raspberries. Add orange juice, crushed pineapple with juice, lemon juice, and a few drops of red food coloring, if desired. Pour into shallow pan and freeze. Remove from freezer one hour before serving. Break up with fork till slushy. Fill punch cups two-thirds full with slush. Pour carbonated lemon-lime beverage over slush. Makes 20 half-cup servings.

SPICED CRANBERRY COCKTAIL

4 cups (1 32-ounce bottle) cranberry
  juice cocktail
2 cups orange juice
1 cup unsweetened grapefruit juice
½ cup grenadine syrup
¼ teaspoon ground cloves
¼ teaspoon ground nutmeg

Combine ingredients and heat till warm. Makes 15 half-cup servings.

WARM ORANGE ALMOND DRINK

3 cups sugar
4 cups water
1 12-ounce can frozen orange juice,
*   undiluted*
1½ cups lemon juice
1 tablespoon almond flavoring
2 teaspoons vanilla
¼ teaspoon each ground cloves,
*   allspice, and cinnamon (optional)*
4 quarts water

Heat sugar and 4 cups water in a pan large enough to hold six quarts. Add remaining ingredients and heat till hot. Do not boil. Serve warm. Leftover beverage can be cooled and stored in refrigerator for ten days. Makes 48 half-cup servings.

LIME SLUSH PUNCH

2 cups sugar
8 cups water
1 12-ounce can frozen limeade
5 fresh limes, juiced
2 12-ounce lemon-lime carbonated
*   beverage*

Combine sugar and water and heat slightly till dissolved. Add frozen limeade and juice of 5 limes. Mix and pour into shallow pan. Freeze. (Can be kept in freezer up to three months.) Remove from freezer about an hour before serving and break up into slush. Pour into punch bowl and add carbonated lemon-lime beverage. Makes 18 half-cup servings.

HOT TOMATO ZIP

1 46-ounce can tomato juice
1 46-ounce can vegetable juice cocktail
2 10-ounce cans consommé, undiluted
1 10-ounce can tomato soup
1 soup can water
1 teaspoon seasoned salt
½ teaspoon onion salt
Thin lemon slices

Combine all ingredients except lemon slices in saucepan and heat. Serve warm, garnished with lemon slices. Makes 32 half-cup servings.

SHRIMP COCKTAIL BEVERAGE

2 46-ounce cans tomato juice
1½ cups catsup
1 cup celery, chopped fine
3 tablespoons sugar
2 cans (4½ ounces each) cleaned
    broken shrimp, drained
3 tablespoons Worcestershire sauce
2 tablespoons prepared horseradish
    sauce
Juice of 1 lemon
½ teaspoon salt
½ teaspoon garlic salt

Mix ingredients together in gallon container. Refrigerate several hours or overnight. Serve cold. Makes 25 half-cup servings.

SANTA CLAUS PUNCH

2 packages unsweetened raspberry
   punch powder
1 cup sugar
4 cups cranberry juice cocktail
12 cups (3 quarts) crushed ice and
   water

Combine punch mix with sugar. Add cranberry juice and stir till dissolved. Mix in crushed ice and water. Makes 32 half-cup servings.

RASPBERRY SLUSH FOR A CROWD

3 packets unsweetened raspberry
   punch powder
4 cups sugar
4 cups warm water
1 46-ounce can pineapple juice
1 12-ounce can frozen lemonade
1 6-ounce can frozen lemon juice
3 10-ounce packages frozen
   raspberries
1 2-liter bottle carbonated lemon-lime
   beverage

In a 2-gallon container, dissolve raspberry punch mix and sugar in warm water. Add pineapple juice, lemonade, lemon juice, and raspberries and enough water (about 3½ quarts) to make 2 gallons. Stir till blended. Pour into large freezer containers and freeze. When ready to serve, thaw till slushy. Pour into punch bowl or individual punch cups and add carbonated lemon-lime beverage. Makes 75 half-cup servings.

FRUIT PUNCH CONCENTRATE

9 cups sugar
6 packets unsweetened orange punch
powder
6 packets unsweetened cherry punch
powder
1 46-ounce can orange juice
1 46-ounce can pineapple juice

Mix sugar and punch mixes. Add orange juice and pineapple juice. Stir till dissolved. Store in refrigerator. When ready to serve, mix one part concentrate to four parts water. Makes 5 gallons when diluted.

HOT CRAB BITES

9 slices white bread
1 cup crabmeat or imitation crab,
flaked
1 small onion, grated
1 cup grated Cheddar cheese
1 cup mayonnaise
½ teaspoon salt
Sliced olives and sprigs of parsley for
garnish

Remove crusts from bread slices. Combine crabmeat, onion, cheese, mayonnaise, and salt. Spread on bread slices. Cut each slice into fourths, in choice of strips, squares, or triangles. Place on a cookie sheet sprayed with cooking spray. Broil till bubbly and golden. Garnish each piece with an olive slice and a sprig of parsley. Makes 36 appetizers.

SWEET AND SOUR CHICKEN STRIPS

8 boneless chicken breasts
1 egg
1½ cups cold water
1 cup flour
½ cup cornstarch
1 teaspoon baking powder
½ teaspoon salt
¼ teaspoon black pepper
Additional flour for dipping
Shortening for deep-fat frying
1 cup sugar
2 tablespoons cornstarch
½ cup vinegar
½ cup catsup
1 8-ounce can crushed pineapple and
*   juice*
1 cup pineapple juice

Skin chicken and cut on an angle into ½-inch strips. Make tempura batter by beating egg and water. Beat in flour, ½ cup cornstarch, baking powder, salt, and pepper. Dip chicken strips in flour, then in batter. Deep-fry for 2 to 3 minutes. Drain on paper towels. Make sauce by mixing sugar and 2 tablespoons cornstarch in saucepan; add remaining ingredients. Cook and stir till thickened. Serve as dip for chicken strips. Makes 8 to 10 servings.

PARTY DEVILED EGGS

6 hard-cooked eggs
¼ cup mayonnaise
1 teaspoon vinegar
1 teaspoon prepared mustard
⅛ teaspoon salt
Dash of white pepper
⅛ teaspoon Worcestershire sauce
1 drop red pepper sauce (optional)

Peel eggs; cut in half lengthwise. Slip out yolks; mash with fork. Add remaining ingredients to mashed yolks and mix till well blended. Spoon into egg-white halves. Sprinkle with paprika and garnish with pimiento and parsley, if desired. Makes 12 deviled eggs.

GUACAMOLE

2 large ripe avocados
1 tablespoon finely chopped green onion
½ teaspoon salt
Dash of oregano
1½ tablespoons lemon juice
Few drops red pepper sauce (optional)
Chopped jalapeno peppers (optional)

Peel avocados and remove stones. Place in small bowl and mash with fork. Add green onion, salt, and oregano; mash together thoroughly. Add lemon juice and mix again. For hot guacamole, add red pepper sauce or jalapeno peppers according to taste. Makes about 1⅓ cups.

GLAZED MEATBALLS

3 slices bread
⅔ cup milk
2 eggs, beaten
1½ pounds ground beef
1 tablespoon dijon mustard
½ teaspoon salt
½ teaspoon pepper
Sweet-Sour Glaze (below)
Hot, fluffy cooked rice (optional)

Preheat oven to 450 degrees F. Soak bread in milk till soft. Add eggs, ground beef, and seasonings; mix till well blended. Shape into ¾-inch or 1-inch balls; place on shallow baking sheets and bake 10 to 15 minutes. (Meatballs may be made to this point, then refrigerated till shortly before serving time.)

Heat meatballs in Sweet-Sour Glaze. Serve in chafing dish with toothpicks to spear the meatballs, or as a main course with hot, fluffy rice. Makes about 100 ¾-inch or 50 1-inch meatballs (25 servings).

SWEET-SOUR GLAZE

1½ cups chicken broth
¾ cup pineapple chunks
2 green peppers, cut in chunks
4 tablespoons cornstarch
1 tablespoon soy sauce
¾ cup wine vinegar
¾ cup sugar

Heat chicken broth, pineapple chunks, and green pepper chunks in saucepan and simmer 5 minutes. Mix remaining ingredients and add to hot broth. Cook and stir till thickened.

HONEY YOGURT DIP

1 16-ounce carton cottage cheese
½ cup plain yogurt
¼ cup honey
½ cup grated coconut
2 teaspoons grated orange rind

Blend cottage cheese and yogurt in food processor or blender till smooth.

Stir in remaining ingredients; chill. Serve as dip for fresh fruit.

BROILED MUSHROOM APPETIZERS

CRAB FILLING

1 pound fresh mushrooms
2 tablespoons margarine
1 can (7½ ounces) crabmeat,
    drained and flaked
1 cup prepared instant mashed
    potatoes
1 cup shredded Cheddar cheese
2 teaspoons lemon juice
1 teaspoon seasoned salt

Wash mushrooms and remove stems. Chop stems and sauté in 2 tablespoons margarine. Add remaining ingredients; mix well and spoon into mushroom caps. Place on baking sheet and broil till lightly browned. Makes about 30 appetizers.

BACON-CHIVE FILLING

½ pound fresh mushrooms
½ pound bacon
2 to 3 tablespoons cream cheese
2 tablespoons minced green
    onion

Wash mushrooms and remove stems; use stems for another purpose. Sauté bacon till brown; drain and crumble. Mix with softened cream cheese and green onion. Fill mushroom caps; place on baking sheet and broil till lightly browned. Makes about 15 appetizers.

ONION-CHEESE FILLING

½ pound fresh mushrooms
1 3-ounce package cream
    cheese, softened
3 tablespoons fine dry bread
    crumbs
2 tablespoons finely chopped
    fresh parsley
2 teaspoons grated fresh onion
¼ teaspoon paprika
¼ teaspoon salt

Wash mushrooms and remove stems; use stems for another purpose. Mix remaining ingredients and fill each mushroom cap. Place on baking sheet and broil till lightly browned. Makes about 15 appetizers.

TANGY PARTY DIP

1 8-ounce package cream cheese, softened
¼ cup mayonnaise
½ teaspoon red pepper sauce
1 teaspoon Worcestershire sauce
4 green onions, finely chopped
1 teaspoon seasoned salt
½ teaspoon paprika
1 3½-ounce package thinly sliced beef

Whip cream cheese and mayonnaise. Add seasonings. Finely chop beef and blend into cream-cheese mixture. Serve as a dip for fresh vegetables or as a spread for crackers. Makes 1¼ cups.

MARINATED MUSHROOMS

1 pound fresh mushrooms
1 cup vinegar
1 cup oil
2 cloves garlic, minced
3 tablespoons minced fresh parsley
3 tablespoon minced green onions
1 teaspoon sugar
1 teaspoon salt

Wash and dry mushrooms. Blend remaining ingredients and pour over mushrooms. Cover and marinate in refrigerator overnight. Drain. Serve as appetizer, or spoon on top of salad greens and serve as a salad.

SANDWICH ROLLS

1 large loaf sliced white sandwich bread
1 can (6½ ounces) tuna fish, drained
¼ cup minced celery
2 green onions, minced
1 tablespoon sweet pickle relish
¼ cup mayonnaise
Butter or margarine, softened
Mayonnaise and chopped parsley to dip
    sandwich-roll ends
1 3-ounce package cream cheese, softened
Green and yellow food coloring

Trim crusts from bread to make 4x4-inch slices. Mix tuna, celery, green onions, pickle relish, and ¼ cup mayonnaise till well blended. Flatten bread slices with rolling pin. Spread with butter or margarine, then thin layer of filling. Roll each slice into a tight roll. Dip ends in mayonnaise and then chopped parsley; place seam down on a tray. Tint half of cream cheese yellow and half green. Fill pastry bags with tinted cream cheese and decorate top of each sandwich with a flower and leaf, using star and leaf tips. Cover sandwiches with plastic wrap or store in a covered container and refrigerate till ready to serve. Makes 25 sandwich rolls.

DILLY DIP

1 cup sour cream
1 cup mayonnaise
1 teaspoon Worcestershire sauce
1 tablespoon dill weed
1 tablespoon finely chopped green onions
1 tablespoon Bon Appetit

Mix ingredients together till well blended. Cover and refrigerate several hours or overnight. Makes 2 cups. Serve with fresh vegetables.

FESTIVE CHEESE BALL

2 8-ounce packages cream cheese
2 cups grated sharp cheese
2 tablespoons finely chopped green
 onions
2 teaspoons Worcestershire sauce
1 teaspoon lemon juice
½ teaspoon lemon pepper
1 cup finely chopped nuts
Chopped parsley

Soften cream cheese. Add remaining ingredients except nuts and parsley; mix till well blended. Dividing mixture in half, spoon into 2 small bowls lined with wax paper. Refrigerate for several hours. Lift out wax paper with cheese mixture from each bowl, and mold cheese into ball, using wax paper to protect hands. Roll each ball in chopped nuts and parsley. Refrigerate. Remove about 15 minutes before serving and serve with a variety of crackers. Makes 2 small balls.

FRUIT DIP

2 8-ounce packages cream cheese,
 softened
1 16-ounce jar marshmallow creme
2 tablespoons frozen orange juice
 concentrate
1 teaspoon minced fresh ginger
 (optional)

Whip softened cream cheese with marshmallow creme and orange juice concentrate. Add fresh ginger, if desired. Use as dip for fresh fruit.

LIVER PATÉ

1 pound pork liver
¾ pound pork sausage
1 onion
2 tablespoons flour
2 tablespoons butter
2 cups milk
¾ teaspoon pepper
1½ teaspoons salt
½ teaspoon allspice
¼ teaspoon cloves
2 eggs
Pickled beets

Preheat oven to 350 degrees F. Put liver, pork sausage, and onions through meat grinder two times. Set aside while you prepare white sauce: In a saucepan, melt butter; stir in flour, then milk, and cook, stirring constantly, till thickened. Add white sauce to ground liver mixture and mix well. Stir in seasonings and eggs and mix well. Pour mixture into greased loaf pan. Place loaf pan in a shallow pan of water and bake 1¼ hours. Cool. Spread on bread or crackers and garnish with piece of pickled beet.

CHICKEN ALMOND PUFFS

½ cup butter or margarine
1 cup chicken broth
1 cup flour
¼ teaspoon salt
4 eggs
1 cup finely diced cooked chicken
3 tablespoons finely chopped almonds

Preheat oven to 400 degrees F. In saucepan on top of stove, heat butter and chicken stock. When butter is melted, add flour and salt, and stir vigorously with wooden spoon till mixture forms ball. Remove from heat. Beat eggs in, one at a time, and continue beating till dough thickens. Stir in chicken and almonds. Drop by teaspoon onto greased baking sheet. Bake 15 minutes or till brown. Makes 4 dozen cocktail puffs.

PINEAPPLE CHEESE ROLL

2 8-ounce packages cream cheese
1 can (8½ ounces) crushed pineapple,
  drained
2 tablespoons finely chopped green
  onions
¼ cup minced green pepper
1 tablespoon seasoned salt
1 cup chopped pecans

Soften cream cheese. Press all juice out of pineapple (use juice for another purpose) and combine pineapple with cream cheese, onions, minced green pepper, and seasoned salt. Mix well with wooden spoon. Refrigerate for several hours. Shape into a log and roll in chopped pecans. Refrigerate till ready to serve. Makes 1 roll.

BACON-CHESTNUT TIDBITS

1 pound bacon
2 cans whole water chestnuts
1 cup catsup
½ cup sugar

Preheat oven to 375 degrees F. Cut each bacon strip into four pieces. Wrap each piece of bacon around a water chestnut and secure with a toothpick. Place on cookie sheet and bake for 10 minutes. Drain and place bacon-wrapped tidbits in casserole dish. Mix catsup and sugar and pour over top of tidbits. Cover and bake for 15 minutes more. Makes 72 pieces.

Variation: In place of catsup and sugar mixture, use favorite commercial or homemade barbecue sauce.

SHRIMP PLATTER APPETIZER

1 8-ounce package cream cheese, softened
½ cup sour cream
¼ cup mayonnaise
2 cans (4¼ ounces each) broken shrimp,
* rinsed and drained*
1 cup seafood cocktail sauce
2 cups shredded Mozzarella cheese
1 green pepper, chopped
3 green onions, chopped
1 large tomato, diced

Combine cream cheese, sour cream, and mayonnaise. Spread on a 12-inch glass plate. Scatter shrimp over the cheese layer. Cover with cocktail sauce. Then add a layer of shredded Mozzarella cheese, a layer of green peppers, and a layer of green onions. Arrange diced tomato in the center. Cover with plastic wrap and chill. Serve with assorted crackers.

VEGETABLE CURRY DUNK

1 cup sour cream
1 cup mayonnaise
¼ cup finely chopped green onions
¼ cup chopped green peppers
2 tablespoons shredded carrot
2 teaspoons curry powder
¼ teaspoon black pepper

Blend all ingredients in food processor or blender till smooth; chill for several hours. Makes 2½ cups dip. Serve with fresh vegetables.

WARMING SOUPS

HEARTY TURKEY VEGETABLE SOUP

2 quarts turkey broth
1 cup cubed potatoes
1 cup sliced carrots
1 cup sliced celery
¼ cup chopped onions
1 teaspoon salt
Pepper to taste
1 cup uncooked noodles
2 cups cooked turkey meat, cut up
1 cup frozen peas

Prepare broth: Strip as much turkey meat as possible from bones of roast turkey; refrigerate meat. Place bones and skin into a large stock pot and barely cover with water. Add a small sliced carrot, a chopped onion, a few celery leaves, 2 teaspoons salt, and a bay leaf. Cover and simmer for 2 to 3 hours. Strain broth. Use broth immediately, or refrigerate and use within 2 days, or freeze.

Prepare soup: Add to turkey broth the potatoes, carrots, celery, onions, salt, and pepper. Bring to boil. Add noodles; simmer 30 minutes. Add turkey and peas; heat thoroughly and serve. Makes 8 servings.

PEASANT SOUP

1 cup Great Northern beans
3 cups water
1 teaspoon salt
1 ham hock (or ½ pound salt pork or diced ham)
3 carrots, peeled and diced
1 onion, chopped
1 cup chopped celery
2 cups chopped cabbage
½ teaspoon garlic powder
½ teaspoon black pepper
1 teaspoon taco seasoning
¼ cup ham base seasoning
4 cups water

Cover beans with water and soak overnight (or bring to boil for 2 minutes; remove from heat and let stand for 1 hour). Drain. Combine with 3 cups water, salt, and ham hock. Cover and simmer about 2 hours or till beans are tender. Add diced carrots, chopped onion, chopped celery, chopped cabbage, remaining seasonings, and 4 cups water. Simmer till vegetables are tender. Remove ham hock and cut meat off bone. Dice meat and return to soup. Makes 8 servings.

CREAM OF LEEK SOUP

*4 cups chicken stock (or 4 cups water
  and ¼ cup chicken base)
3 large leeks (about 3 cups chopped)
1 cup chopped celery
1 cup chopped onions
6 potatoes, cooked, peeled, and cubed
1 bay leaf
1 teaspoon salt
Black pepper to taste
3 cups milk
¼ cup butter or margarine
¼ cup flour*

Heat chicken stock in large saucepan. Trim green tops from leeks within 2 inches of white part. Wash thoroughly and coarsely chop. Add leeks, celery, onions, potatoes, bay leaf, salt, and pepper to chicken stock and simmer till vegetables are tender. Add milk and heat. Melt butter in a heavy saucepan, and stir in flour to make roux. Add to soup and stir till thickened. Makes 8 to 10 servings.

VICHYSSOISE

Follow recipe for Cream of Leek Soup. Press vegetables through sieve. Add 3 cups of half and half instead of milk. Season with ½ teaspoon nutmeg. Chill several hours. Serve cold, garnished with whipped cream and snipped chives.

LION HOUSE OYSTER STEW

3 tablespoons margarine
3 tablespoons flour
2 cups milk
2 cups light cream
2 8-ounce cans oysters and juice
½ teaspoon salt
¼ teaspoon black pepper

Melt margarine in heavy saucepan, and stir in flour to make roux. Gradually add milk and light cream; cook and stir till thickened. Add oysters with juice and seasonings. Heat slowly to simmer point. Serve when oysters are hot—do not boil. Makes 6 servings.

TACO SOUP

1 pound ground beef
1 medium onion, chopped
1 package mild taco seasoning mix
1 16-ounce can cut corn
1 16-ounce can kidney beans, drained
   and rinsed
1 28-ounce can stewed tomatoes
1 8-ounce can tomato sauce
Tortilla chips
Grated cheese

Brown ground beef in heavy saucepan. Drain. Sauté chopped onion; add to ground beef. Stir in taco seasoning, corn, kidney beans, stewed tomatoes, and tomato sauce. Simmer for 20 to 30 minutes. Serve topped with tortilla chips and grated cheese. Makes 8 servings.

SEAFOOD BISQUE

1½ to 2 cups cooked fish (halibut,
*   salmon, cod, or other)*
½ cup cooked shrimp
¼ cup butter
½ cup diced celery
¼ cup minced green onion
3 tablespoons flour
2 cups milk
1 cup light cream
1 cup fish stock or clam juice
1 teaspoon salt
4 drops red pepper sauce
⅛ teaspoon black pepper
1 teaspoon savory salt
Minced parsley for garnish

Shred fish and shrimp with fork and set aside. Melt butter in saucepan. Add celery and onion; sauté. Add flour and stir till blended. Gradually add milk, cream, and fish stock or clam juice. Stir till slightly thickened. Add fish, salt, red pepper sauce, pepper, and savory salt. Simmer for a few minutes to blend flavors; do not boil. Garnish each serving with minced parsley. Makes 6 servings.

VEGETABLE CHEESE CHOWDER

4 cups cubed potatoes
2 cups diced carrots
2 cups chopped celery
½ cup minced onions
2 teaspoons salt
4 cups water
1 10-ounce package frozen broccoli
3 tablespoons chicken base
3½ cups milk
½ cup margarine
½ cup flour
1 tablespoon dry mustard
1 pound processed American cheese

Prepare potatoes, carrots, celery, and onions. Place in large soup pot and add salt and water. Cook till vegetables are tender, about 20 minutes. Add broccoli, chicken base, and milk. Simmer for 5 more minutes. In separate pan, melt margarine and add flour and dry mustard; stir to make roux. Add to soup and stir till thickened. Cut cheese into cubes and add to soup. Stir till cheese is melted. Keep hot, but do not boil, till ready to serve. Makes 8 to 10 servings.

FRENCH ONION SOUP

3 cups sliced onions
¼ cup butter
2 cups beef stock (or 2 cups water
and 2 tablespoons beef base)
2 cups chicken stock (or 2 cups water
and 2 tablespoons chicken base)
1 teaspoon salt
¼ teaspoon pepper
¼ cup grape juice
Parmesan Toast Cubes

Sauté sliced onions in melted butter till golden brown. Add beef stock, chicken stock, salt, and pepper. Add grape juice and simmer for 30 minutes. Ladle into bowls and top with Parmesan Toast Cubes (recipe below) just before serving. Makes 4 servings.

PARMESAN TOAST CUBES

Slice French bread into thick slices. Spread with butter and sprinkle with Parmesan cheese. Place under broiler and toast till light brown. Remove and cut into large cubes.

CREAM OF ASPARAGUS SOUP

1 15-ounce can asparagus*
3 tablespoons margarine
¼ cup minced onions
3 tablespoons flour
1 15-ounce can chicken broth
1 cup milk
¼ teaspoon paprika
½ teaspoon salt

Pour asparagus and liquid into blender and whirl till puréed. Melt margarine in heavy saucepan. Add onions and sauté till soft. Stir in flour. Add puréed asparagus, chicken broth, milk, paprika, and salt. Stir and cook till slightly thickened. Makes 6 servings.

*Note: If using fresh asparagus, simmer three-fourths pound fresh cleaned asparagus in 2 cups salted water till tender. Cool slightly and purée in blender. Follow recipe as above.

CHICKEN-RICE SOUP

2½ to 3 pound broiler-fryer chicken
4 cups water
1 carrot, cut in chunks
1 onion, cut in chunks
1 celery stalk, cut in chunks
1 teaspoon salt
1 clove garlic, crushed
1 cup cooked rice
2 fresh tomatoes, cut into wedges
½ cup green pepper, chopped
1 medium onion, chopped
1 cup frozen green peas
¼ cup sliced pimiento-stuffed olives

Place chicken, water, carrot, onion, celery, salt, and garlic in large kettle and simmer for 1 hour. Remove chicken from broth. Strain vegetables from broth and discard; cool broth and skim off fat. Cool chicken slightly and remove bones and skin. Cut chicken in pieces. Stir chicken and remaining ingredients into broth. Heat uncovered till hot, about 10 minutes. Makes 8 servings.

BROCCOLI-CHEESE SOUP

1½ pounds fresh broccoli or 2 10-ounce
  packages frozen chopped broccoli
3 tablespoons margarine
¼ cup chopped onion
3 tablespoons flour
2 cups chicken broth (or 2 cups water
  and 2 tablespoons chicken base)
2 cups light cream
1 teaspoon salt
¼ teaspoon nutmeg
1 cup grated Cheddar cheese

Wash and chop broccoli. Cook in small amount of salted water till tender. Melt margarine in heavy saucepan. Add onion and cook till clear. Stir in flour to make roux; slowly add broth and cream. Stir and cook till thickened. Add salt, nutmeg, and cooked broccoli. Just before serving, stir in cheese. Makes 6 servings.

FESTIVE SALADS

MOLDED FRESH CRANBERRY SALAD

2 cups water
¾ cup sugar
1 12-ounce package fresh cranberries
1 6-ounce package orange gelatin
1 can (8¼ ounces) crushed pineapple and juice
½ cup chopped celery
Sour cream and orange slices for garnish

Heat water, sugar, and cranberries in saucepan and boil 5 minutes. Stir in gelatin till dissolved. Add pineapple with juice and celery. Pour into 8 individual molds. Refrigerate till firm, at least 6 hours. Unmold on salad greens. Garnish each serving with sour cream and an orange slice. Makes 8 servings.

PANTRY HEALTH SALAD

1 head romaine lettuce
¼ pound mushrooms
1 cup fresh bean sprouts
1 carrot, peeled and sliced thin
½ cup peanuts
½ cup sunflower seeds
1 cup shredded Cheddar cheese
4 hard-cooked eggs, peeled and sliced
1 avocado, peeled and sliced

Wash romaine and tear into bite-size pieces into large bowl. Wash and dry mushrooms and slice. Rinse bean sprouts; drain well. Add mushrooms, bean sprouts, and carrot slices to romaine. Add peanuts, sunflower seeds, and shredded cheese and toss lightly. Garnish with sliced egg and avocado. Serve with favorite dressing. Makes 8 to 10 servings.

ORANGE FRUIT SLAW

3 cups shredded cabbage
1 orange, peeled and sectioned
1 cup halved seedless red grapes
½ cup sliced celery
1 apple, cored and chopped
1 8-ounce carton orange yogurt
¼ cup toasted slivered almonds

Combine cabbage, orange sections, grapes, celery, and apple in salad bowl. Mix in orange yogurt. Chill. Just before serving, garnish with toasted slivered almonds.

SEAFOOD PASTA SALAD

8 ounces pasta spirals
2 cups diced Provolone or Cheddar cheese
2 small carrots, thinly sliced
1 small zucchini, quartered and sliced
1 cup sliced mushrooms
¾ cup bias-cut celery
½ cup thinly sliced radishes
¼ cup chopped red onion
1 small green pepper, cut in 1-inch strips
½ cup black olives, cut in half
2 cups imitation crabmeat
1 7-ounce carton clam dip
Salt and pepper to taste

Cook pasta. Drain and chill. Prepare the cheese, vegetables, and olives and place in large bowl with pasta. Add crabmeat and clam dip; mix till blended. Add salt and pepper. Refrigerate till ready to serve. Makes 10 to 12 servings.

TORTELLINI PRIMAVERA

1 8-ounce package tortellini
2 stalks broccoli, cut into flowerets
3 carrots, peeled and sliced
½ cup chopped green onions
½ cup chopped red pepper
½ cup chopped green pepper
½ cup mayonnaise
1 teaspoon grated orange rind
½ teaspoon thyme
1 teaspoon basil
1 teaspoon salt
¼ teaspoon black pepper
Leaf lettuce
Shredded Mozzarella cheese for garnish

Cook tortellini in boiling, salted water about 15 minutes or till tender. Drain and cool under cold running water. Steam broccoli and sliced carrots till tender crisp. Cool under cold running water. Combine tortellini, broccoli, carrots, green onions, and red and green peppers. Mix mayonnaise, orange rind, and seasonings. Pour over tortellini mixture. Toss to coat.

For each serving line a salad plate with lettuce. Spoon on a mound of salad mixture. Sprinkle with 1 tablespoon shredded cheese. Serve chilled or at room temperature. Makes 8 servings.

LION HOUSE BUFFET SALAD

1 small head iceberg lettuce
1 small head romaine lettuce
2 large tomatoes, diced
2 avocados, diced
¼ cup chopped green onions
4 hard-cooked eggs, peeled and sliced
½ pound cooked bacon pieces
6 slices American processed cheese,
  sliced into thin strips
½ cup sliced black olives
1 cup Italian salad dressing

Wash iceberg lettuce and romaine and tear into bite-size pieces in large bowl. Add tomatoes, avocados, green onions, eggs, bacon pieces, cheese, and olives. Keep chilled till ready to serve. Just before serving, add dressing and toss lightly to combine. Makes 8 to 10 servings.

RICE-SHRIMP SALAD

1 cup uncooked rice
2 cups water
1 teaspoon salt
2 cups cooked salad shrimp
1 small can pimiento, diced
2 tablespoons chopped green onion
1 small green pepper, chopped
1 small carrot, chopped
1 10-ounce package green peas,
  cooked and drained
1 cup mayonnaise
1 teaspoon seasoned salt
¼ teaspoon pepper

Cook rice, water, and salt in covered saucepan for 20 minutes or till rice is done. Cool. Mix with remaining ingredients till blended. Cover and refrigerate for several hours or overnight.

To serve, scoop onto lettuce leaf. Makes 6 to 8 servings.

FIVE-WAY CRAB SALAD

8 ounces imitation crabmeat
½ cup sliced celery
¼ cup chopped green onions
1 tomato, cubed
¼ cup sliced ripe olives
3 hard-cooked eggs, peeled and
  chopped
½ cup mayonnaise
1 teaspoon seasoned salt
½ teaspoon mustard
Salt and pepper to taste

Combine crabmeat with celery, onions, tomato, olives, and chopped egg. Gently blend in mayonnaise and seasonings. Chill. Makes 4 to 5 cups salad. Serve in any of the following ways:

1. *Stuffed Avocado:* Cut 4 avocadoes in half; remove pit. Scoop crab salad into center of cavity. Makes 8 stuffed avocadoes.

2. *Stuffed Tomato:* Cut tomatoes into 8 sections, leaving connected at bottom. Place each tomato on lettuce leaf and scoop crab salad into center of each. Fills 6 to 8 tomatoes.

3. *Croissant Sandwiches:* Slice croissants and stuff with crab salad. Makes 6 to 8 croissant sandwiches.

4. *Crab puffs:* Cut tops off cocktail-size cream puffs. Spoon crab salad into each puff and garnish with sprig of parsley. Fills 20 to 24 puffs.

5. *Entrée Salad:* Line large salad plate with green leafy lettuce. Place mound of shredded lettuce in center. Spoon crab salad on top of lettuce. Garnish with lemon wedge, olives, tomato wedges, and parsley. Makes 6 large salads.

ORIENTAL CABBAGE SLAW WITH CHICKEN

2 cups diced cooked chicken
4 cups shredded cabbage
1 package chicken-flavored ramen
*   noodles*
4 green onions, sliced
2 tablespoons sesame seeds
¼ cup vinegar
¼ cup salad oil
2 tablespoons sugar
½ teaspoon salt
1 flavoring packet from ramen
*   noodles*
½ cup slivered almonds

Place chicken and cabbage in mixing bowl. Break noodles up and place in colander. Pour boiling water over to soften slightly. Add to cabbage with onions and sesame seeds. Combine vinegar, salad oil, sugar, salt, and contents of flavoring packet. Pour over cabbage, mixing well. Cover and refrigerate overnight or for several hours. Just before serving, stir in slivered almonds. Makes 6 to 8 servings.

ANGIE EARL'S FROZEN FRUIT SALAD

1 pint whipping cream
1 cup mayonnaise
¼ cup powdered sugar
3 tablespoons lemon juice
¼ teaspoon salt
½ cup chopped nuts
1 cup crushed pineapple, drained
½ cup maraschino cherries, chopped
1 cup fruit cocktail, drained

Whip cream stiff; blend in mayonnaise, powdered sugar, lemon juice, and salt. Pour into loaf pan; place in freezer and partially freeze. Remove from freezer, return to bowl, and fold in nuts, pineapple, maraschino cherries, and fruit cocktail. Pour back into pan and freeze. Let stand in freezer several days to ripen. To serve, cut into slices and serve on a lettuce leaf. Makes 8 servings.

STRAWBERRY NUT SALAD

1 6-ounce package strawberry gelatin
1 cup boiling water
1 10-ounce package frozen, sliced strawberries,
  thawed but undrained
1 20-ounce can crushed pineapple, with juice
3 medium bananas, peeled and mashed
½ cup walnuts, coarsely chopped
1 16-ounce carton sour cream

Dissolve gelatin in boiling water. Fold in strawberries, drained pineapple, mashed bananas, and nuts. Pour one-half of mixture into 8x12-inch pan. Refrigerate till firm. Whip sour cream, then spread on set gelatin. Gently spoon remainder of gelatin mixture on top. Refrigerate. Serves 8 to 10.

CHRISTMAS EGGNOG SALAD

1 envelope unflavored gelatin
1 8-ounce can crushed pineapple and
*   juice*
2 tablespoons lemon juice
1½ cups dairy eggnog
½ cup finely chopped celery
1½ cups cranberry juice cocktail or
*   apple juice*
1 3-ounce package raspberry gelatin
1 14-ounce jar (1¾ cups) cranberry-
*   orange relish*
Frosted cranberries for garnish

In small saucepan, soften unflavored gelatin in undrained crushed pineapple for 5 minutes. Add lemon juice. Cook and stir over medium heat till gelatin dissolves. Stir in eggnog and celery and pour into 12x7x2-inch pan. Chill till almost firm. Heat cranberry juice to boiling. Add raspberry gelatin and stir till dissolved. Fold in cranberry-orange relish. Chill till partially set; then pour over eggnog mixture. Chill till firm. Cut into squares. Garnish with frosted cranberries. Makes 12 servings.

LEMON SHRIMP GELATIN

1 6-ounce package lemon gelatin
1 teaspoon salt
1 cup boiling water
¾ cup cold water
½ cup cream, whipped
½ cup salad dressing
3 hard-cooked eggs, peeled and chopped
1 cup cooked salad shrimp
1 cup chopped celery
¼ cup chopped green pepper
4 green onions, minced
½ cup grated Cheddar cheese
½ cup chopped walnuts

Dissolve gelatin and salt in boiling water. Add cold water and refrigerate till partially set. Remove from refrigerator and whip till foamy. Mix in whipped cream and salad dressing. Add chopped eggs, shrimp, celery, green pepper, onions, cheese, and walnuts. Pour into 1-quart mold and refrigerate 12 hours or overnight. Makes 8 servings.

POPPY SEED SPINACH TOSS

½ cup red wine vinegar
¾ cup salad oil
2 teaspoons poppy seeds
4 tablespoons sugar
1 tablespoon minced Bermuda onion
1 teaspoon salt
½ teaspoon dry mustard
1 pound fresh spinach
½ head iceberg lettuce
1 cup shredded Swiss cheese
1 cup cottage cheese or ricotta cheese
½ pound fresh mushrooms, cleaned
   and sliced
½ Bermuda onion, sliced thin and
   separated into rings
2 hard-cooked eggs, peeled and
   chopped

Prepare dressing: Pour vinegar and oil in blender. Add poppy seeds, sugar, minced Bermuda onion, salt, and dry mustard. Whirl for a few seconds to blend. Or place ingredients in a pint jar and shake. Refrigerate. Flavor improves if dressing is made several hours in advance.

Prepare salad: Wash spinach, dry thoroughly, and discard stems. Tear in pieces into large salad bowl. Tear lettuce in pieces into bowl. Add Swiss cheese, cottage cheese, mushrooms, onion rings, and chopped eggs. When ready to serve, pour over dressing and toss to coat greens. Serve immediately. Makes 8 servings.

CHRISTMAS RAINBOW SALAD

1 6-ounce package red gelatin
1 cup boiling water
1 cup ice water
1 can (15¼ ounces) crushed pineapple
  and juice
1 6-ounce package lemon gelatin
1 cup boiling water
1 cup ice water
½ pint whipping cream, whipped stiff
1 3-ounce package lime gelatin
1 cup boiling water
1 cup ice water

1. Dissolve red gelatin in 1 cup boiling water. Mix in 1 cup ice water and crushed pineapple. Pour into 9x13-inch pan or large mold and refrigerate till set.

2. Dissolve lemon gelatin in 1 cup boiling water. Add 1 cup ice water and refrigerate till syrupy. Whip till foamy, then mix in whipped cream and pour over red gelatin layer. Refrigerate.

3. Dissolve lime gelatin in 1 cup boiling water. Add 1 cup ice water. Pour over lemon layer. Refrigerate. Makes 12 servings.

SUGAR PEA SALAD

1¼ pounds sugar peas
1 cup fresh mushrooms, sliced thin
½ cup finely chopped red bell pepper
1 cup bean sprouts, rinsed and drained
8 ounces cooked shrimp
¼ cup olive oil
1 tablespoon soy sauce
2 tablespoons lemon juice
1 teaspoon brown sugar
2 tablespoons sesame seeds

Cut blossom end from peapods and place in bowl; add mushrooms, red bell pepper, bean sprouts, and shrimp. Combine olive oil, soy sauce, lemon juice, and brown sugar. Pour over vegetables and stir to coat. Cover and refrigerate for several hours, stirring occasionally. To serve, spoon onto lettuce leaf and sprinkle with sesame seeds. Makes 6 to 8 servings.

ORCHARD FRUIT SALAD

Juice and grated peel of 1 orange
2 fresh pears
2 red apples
½ cup fresh or frozen raspberries or
*   blackberries*
¼ cup slivered almonds
Coconut

Grate small amount of peel from orange; then cut and juice orange. Core pears and apples, cut into chunks, and add to orange peel and juice. Gently fold in raspberries or blackberries and slivered almonds. When ready to serve, spoon into a lettuce leaf and sprinkle with coconut.

FRUIT SALAD FOR A CROWD

2 packages (3½ ounces each) instant
    pudding (coconut cream or pistachio)
1 20-ounce can crushed pineapple and juice
1 20-ounce can pineapple tidbits and juice
2 8-ounce cans mandarin oranges, drained
½ cup coconut
2 cups red or green seedless grapes
2 cups miniature marshmallows
1 20-ounce carton frozen whipped
    topping, thawed

In large mixing bowl, mix instant pudding with crushed pineapple and pineapple tidbits and juice. Mix in remaining ingredients till well blended. Cover and refrigerate till ready to serve. Makes 20 to 25 servings.

BUSY-DAY
ENTRÉES

ROAST TURKEY

To buy: When buying turkeys under 12 pounds, allow about ¾ pound per serving. For turkeys 12 pounds and over, allow about ½ pound per serving.

To thaw: If the turkey is frozen, leave in original bag and thaw in refrigerator for 3 to 4 days. Refrigerate or cook as soon as thawed.

To roast: Remove plastic wrap; remove giblets and neck from body cavities. Rinse turkey inside and out, and pat dry with paper towel. Stuff turkey just before roasting—not ahead of time. Fill wishbone area first. Fasten neck skin to back with skewer. Fold wings across back with tips touching. Fill body cavity lightly. Tuck drumsticks under band of skin at tail or tie together with heavy string, then tie to tail. Place turkey breast-side up on rack in shallow roasting pan. Roast uncovered at 325 degrees F. When turkey begins to turn golden, cover with tent of foil to prevent overbrowning.

APPROXIMATE COOKING TIMES FOR READY-TO-COOK TURKEY

8 to 12 pounds: 3 to 4½ hours
12 to 16 pounds: 4½ to 5½ hours
16 to 20 pounds: 5½ to 6½ hours
20 to 24 pounds: 6½ to 7½ hours
Internal Temperature: 185 degrees

To serve: Remove turkey from oven and allow to stand about 20 minutes. Use drippings for gravy. Remove stuffing from turkey. Carve and serve. Refrigerate leftovers as soon as possible after serving.

OLD-FASHIONED SAVORY STUFFING

4 cups diced celery
1 cup chopped onion
1 cup butter or margarine
4 quarts (16 cups) dry bread cubes
1 tablespoon salt
1½ teaspoons poultry seasoning
½ teaspoon sage
½ teaspoon pepper
¾ to 1 cup hot broth or water

Sauté celery and onion in butter. Combine with bread cubes and seasonings; toss lightly. Add enough broth to moisten as desired. Makes enough stuffing for 14- to 18-pound bird.

Giblet Stuffing: Add chopped, cooked giblets; use giblet broth as liquid.

Oyster Stuffing: Add two 8-ounce cans oysters, drained and chopped.

Chestnut Stuffing: Add 1 pound fresh chestnuts. Prepare chestnuts by slashing shells with a sharp knife. Roast on baking sheet at 400 degrees F. for 15 minutes; cool. Peel and coarsely chop chestnuts; then add to stuffing.

PIONEER TURKEY BAKE

2 cups cooked cubed turkey
1 6-ounce package wild rice mix
½ cup chopped celery
2 tablespoons chopped onion
1 4-ounce can sliced mushrooms,
  drained
1 can (10 ounces) cream of chicken
  soup
1 teaspoon Worcestershire sauce
1¼ cups water
¼ cup slivered almonds

Preheat oven to 350 degrees F. Combine turkey with wild rice mix (include contents of seasoning packet) and remaining ingredients. Pour into 1½-quart casserole. Bake covered for 45 minutes. Makes 6 servings.

CHRISTMAS-MORNING CASSEROLE

8 slices bread
¼ cup margarine, melted
1 cup cubed ham
2 cups grated sharp Cheddar cheese
4 eggs, beaten
1½ cups milk
¼ teaspoon salt
¾ teaspoon dry mustard

Preheat oven to 300 degrees F. Remove crusts from bread. Brush on melted margarine. Cut up into cubes and spread into 9x13-inch baking dish. Sprinkle with cubed ham and grated cheese. Mix eggs, milk, salt, and mustard and pour over casserole. Bake for 1½ hours. Makes 8 servings.

CHICKEN DIJON

4 chicken breast halves
¾ cup water
¾ cup white grape juice
1 small onion, sliced
3 tablespoons lemon juice
1 chicken bouillon cube
12 whole peppercorns
1 teaspoon thyme
1 tablespoon honey
2 teaspoons dijon mustard
1½ cups fresh mushrooms, sliced
2 teaspoons flour
2 tablespoons water
Sprigs of fresh thyme and lemon
    slices for garnish

Skin and debone chicken. Place in saucepan and add water, grape juice, onion, lemon juice, bouillon cube, peppercorns, and thyme. Cover and simmer 15 minutes or till done. Remove chicken and keep warm in serving dish. Strain chicken stock and add honey, mustard, and mushrooms. Bring to boil and simmer 10 minutes. Make a paste of flour and water and stir into stock. Stir till slightly thickened. Spoon over chicken. Garnish with sprig of thyme and lemon slice, if desired. Makes 4 servings.

SAVORY BAKED CHICKEN BREASTS

8 chicken breast halves
1 cup sour cream
2 tablespoons lemon juice
1 teaspoon salt
1 teaspoon seasoned salt
1½ teaspoons paprika
1½ teaspoons sage
1½ teaspoons garlic salt
½ teaspoon black pepper
3 cups fine bread crumbs
½ cup butter or margarine, melted

Remove skin from chicken breasts; debone if desired. Combine sour cream and lemon juice. Dip breasts in this mixture and place in covered bowl in refrigerator overnight or at least 4 hours. Preheat oven to 325 degrees F. Combine all seasonings, then mix with bread crumbs. Grease 9x13-inch baking pan. Dip chicken breasts in crumb mixture to coat all sides. Arrange in baking pan. Drizzle melted butter over top. Cover with foil and bake for 2 hours. Remove foil and bake additional 30 minutes to brown. Makes 8 servings.

SWEET AND SOUR CHICKEN

3 pounds chicken breasts
1 teaspoon garlic salt
½ teaspoon black pepper
1 teaspoon monosodium glutamate
  (optional)
1 beaten egg
4 to 6 tablespoons cornstarch or flour
¾ cup sugar
½ cup vinegar
½ cup chicken stock
3½ tablespoons catsup
1 tablespoon soy sauce

Sprinkle chicken with garlic salt, pepper, and monosodium glutamate. Let stand for one hour or more. Preheat oven to 325 degrees F. Dip chicken in beaten egg, then in cornstarch or flour. Brown in hot oil. Place in baking dish. Cover with following sauce: Mix sugar, vinegar, chicken stock, catsup, and soy sauce in saucepan and heat. Pour over chicken. Bake uncovered for 1 hour. Turn chicken once or twice. Makes 6 servings.

CHICKEN CREPES

2 cups cooked chicken, cut in pieces
½ cup shredded cheese
1 15-ounce can pineapple tidbits,
  drained (reverse juice)
½ cup chopped almonds
1 can (10 ounces) cream of chicken
  soup
½ cup pineapple juice
½ teaspoon thyme
½ teaspoon lemon pepper
Chicken Glaze (recipe below)
12 Crepes (page 111)

Preheat oven to 200 degrees F. Mix chicken, cheese, pineapple, and almonds with chicken soup and pineapple juice. Add thyme and lemon pepper and mix ingredients together thoroughly. Place ¼ cup mixture in center of each crepe and roll. Place crepes with seam side down in oiled baking pan. Cover with aluminum foil, and heat in oven for 30 minutes. When ready to serve, arrange two crepes for each serving. Spoon glaze over crepes. Makes 6 servings.

CHICKEN GLAZE

4 tablespoons butter
4 tablespoons flour
3 cups chicken stock
½ teaspoon basil
½ teaspoon rosemary
½ teaspoon rubbed sage

Melt butter in a heavy saucepan. Add flour and stir into paste. Add chicken stock and seasonings and cook till thickened.

A Traditional Christmas Dinner
Roast Turkey with Old-Fashioned Savory Stuffing (page 51),
Molded Fresh Cranberry Salad (page 35),
Deluxe Peas and Celery (page 81)

CHICKEN FAJITAS

6 boneless chicken breasts
1 cup water
1 package fajitas seasoning mix
2 tablespoons salad oil
2 onions, sliced
1 green pepper, sliced in strips
1 red pepper, sliced in strips
12 flour tortillas
Sour cream
Salsa
Guacamole (p. 12)
Fresh lime

Remove skin from chicken breasts; cut breasts into strips. Marinate strips in 1 cup water and the fajitas seasoning mix for two hours. Heat oil in heavy saucepan and sauté onions and green and red peppers till tender crisp. Remove vegetables from pan and add chicken strips, reserving marinade. Sauté chicken till light brown. Add leftover marinade and simmer for five minutes. Return vegetables to pan and heat to mingle flavors. Spoon mixture onto warm tortillas. Fold over and garnish with sour cream, salsa, guacamole, and slice of fresh lime. Makes 6 servings.

SALSA

2 cups chopped tomatoes
1/2 cup chopped onion
1 4-ounce can diced green
    chilies
1 clove garlic, minced
1/2 teaspoon salt
1/4 teaspoon black pepper
1/4 teaspoon cumin
1 tablespoon vinegar
1/4 teaspoon crushed hot
    red pepper (optional)

Mix ingredients till well blended. Cover and refrigerate for at least 2 hours before serving. Or place all ingredients in blender and whirl for a second. The salsa should still be a little chunky, not smooth. Can be refrigerated for up to 1 week.

HOT TURKEY SALAD SUPREME

2 cups diced cooked turkey
2 cups chopped celery
½ teaspoon salt
2 tablespoons minced onion
2 tablespoons lemon juice
1 cup mayonnaise
¾ cup grated cheese
1 cup crushed potato chips
½ cup slivered almonds
Lettuce leaves
Lemon wedges and parsley sprigs for
  garnish

Preheat oven to 350 degrees F. Mix turkey, celery, salt, onion, and lemon juice. Fold in mayonnaise and spoon into greased casserole dish. Sprinkle grated cheese on top, then crushed potato chips, and finally, slivered almonds. Bake for 15 minutes. Don't overbake or mayonnaise will break down. Serve on lettuce leaf and garnish with lemon wedge and parsley. Makes 6 to 8 servings.

HOLIDAY LEG OF LAMB

1 leg of lamb (6 to 7 pounds)
2 cloves garlic, peeled and slivered
1 tablespoon vegetable oil
1 tablespoon rosemary
Salt and pepper to taste

Preheat oven to 375 degrees F. Trim excess fat from lamb. With small knife, make small incisions all over the lamb and insert a sliver of garlic in each. Rub lamb with oil and place in a roasting pan. Rub with rosemary, salt, and pepper. Roast for about 1½ hours or till meat thermometer registers 145 degrees F. for medium-rare or 165 degrees F. for well-done. Makes 8 servings.

MINT SAUCE

2 tablespoons sugar
½ cup white or cider
  vinegar
2 tablespoons water
½ cup minced fresh mint
  leaves

Prepare mint sauce by boiling sugar, vinegar, and water and pouring over mint leaves; steep for 1 hour. Serve with sliced lamb roast.

GINGER BEEF

2 pounds beef round steak
2 cloves garlic
Dash of black pepper
1 can (10 ounces) beef broth
2 tablespoons cornstarch
¼ cup water
1 tablespoon soy sauce
¼ teaspoon crushed fresh gingerroot
1 package frozen Chinese peapods or
  ¾ pound fresh peapods
Hot cooked rice
Cherry tomatoes

Trim fat from meat; cut meat into thin strips. Coat skillet with cooking spray. Peel garlic and make several cuts on end of each clove; cook and stir in skillet till brown. Remove and discard. In skillet in which garlic has been browned, cook meat over medium-high heat till brown, stirring occasionally. Sprinkle with pepper. Stir in broth; heat to boiling. Reduce heat and simmer uncovered till meat is tender, 10 to 15 minutes. (Add small amount of water if necessary.) Mix cornstarch, water, and soy sauce; stir into meat mixture. Cook, stirring constantly, till mixture thickens and boils. Boil and stir 1 minute. Stir in gingerroot and peapods. Cook, stirring occasionally, till peapods are tender crisp, about 5 minutes. Serve on rice. Garnish with cherry tomatoes. Makes 6 to 8 servings.

CABBAGE ROLLS

1 pound lean ground beef
1 cup ground ham
¼ cup chopped onion
¼ cup tomato sauce
½ cup cooked rice
½ teaspoon chili powder
⅛ teaspoon garlic powder
12 outer leaves of cabbage
1 cup tomato sauce
¾ cup grated sharp cheese
½ teaspoon seasoned salt

Brown ground beef. Drain. Add ground ham, onion, ¼ cup tomato sauce, rice, chili powder, and garlic powder. Mix thoroughly. Core cabbage. Remove 12 large outer leaves. Use remainder of cabbage for other recipes. Place leaves in boiling water and simmer for 5 minutes or till tender (leaves should be limp but not overcooked). Drain. Spoon meat mixture into center of each cabbage leaf. Fold up to make a tight roll and place seam down in a baking pan. Mix 1 cup tomato sauce with grated cheese and seasoned salt. Pour over top of cabbage rolls. Keep warm in oven set at 250 degrees F. till ready to serve. Or cover and refrigerate; then bake at 350 degrees F. for 30 minutes. Makes 6 servings.

STUFFED GREEN PEPPERS

6 green bell peppers
1 pound ground beef
1 small onion
½ cup chopped celery
1 can (10½ ounces) cream of
  mushroom soup
½ teaspoon oregano
½ teaspoon chili powder
½ teaspoon basil
½ teaspoon salt
1½ cups cooked rice
1 can (10½ ounces) tomato soup
1 8-ounce can tomato sauce

Preheat oven to 350 degrees F. Cut tops from green peppers; discard seeds. Cook peppers in small amount of boiling water for 5 minutes. Drain and arrange in casserole dish. Brown ground beef and onion. Drain. Add celery, cream of mushroom soup, oregano, chili powder, basil, salt, and rice. Mix well and spoon into green peppers. Combine tomato soup and tomato sauce and pour over top. Bake for 30 minutes. Makes 6 servings.

HEARTY BEEF STEW

2 pounds beef chuck, cut in cubes
2 tablespoons shortening
4 cups water
1 onion, sliced
1 clove garlic
1 tablespoon salt
1 tablespoon lemon juice
1 teaspoon sugar
1 teaspoon Worcestershire sauce
½ teaspoon black pepper
½ teaspoon paprika
2 bay leaves
Dash of allspice
6 carrots, cut in quarters
½ pound small white onions
3 potatoes, peeled and cubed
¼ cup flour

In heavy Dutch oven, slowly brown beef cubes in shortening. Turn often to brown meat on all sides. This should take about 15 minutes. Then add water, onion, garlic (on toothpick so you can retrieve it), salt, lemon juice, sugar, Worcestershire sauce, pepper, paprika, bay leaves, and allspice. Cover with lid and simmer on low heat (do not boil) for 2 hours. Stir occasionally to prevent sticking.

When meat is almost done, add carrots, onions, and potatoes, and simmer for 30 minutes more. Discard bay leaf and garlic. Pour ½ cup water in shaker and add ¼ cup flour; shake to blend. Either remove meat and vegetables from stock or move to one side in pan; stir in flour mixture. Cook and stir till gravy thickens and boils. Makes 8 servings.

PARTY LASAGNE

1½ pounds ground beef
1½ tablespoons oil
1 clove garlic, minced
1 tablespoon parsley flakes
1 tablespoon basil
2 teaspoons salt
1 20-ounce can stewed tomatoes
1 6-ounce can tomato paste
1 10-ounce package lasagne noodles
3 cups large-curd cottage cheese
2 eggs, beaten
½ teaspoon pepper
2 tablespoons parsley flakes
½ cup grated Parmesan cheese
1 pound Mozzarella cheese, thinly
sliced

Brown ground beef in oil. Drain. Add garlic, parsley flakes, basil, and salt. Mix with tomatoes and tomato paste. Simmer, uncovered, till thick, about one hour; stir occasionally. Cook lasagne noodles as directed on package; drain and rinse in cold water. Preheat oven to 375 degrees F. Mix cottage cheese with beaten eggs, pepper, parsley flakes, and Parmesan cheese. Place half of noodles in 9x13-inch baking pan. Spoon on half the cottage cheese mixture. Next place a layer of sliced Mozzarella cheese; then spoon on a layer of meat mixture. Repeat the layers, ending with layer of Mozzarella on top. Bake for 30 minutes. Makes 12 to 15 servings.

CALICO BAKED BEANS

½ to 1 pound ground beef
¾ pound bacon, cut in pieces
1 cup chopped onion
2 20-ounce cans pork and beans
1 16-ounce can kidney beans, drained
1 16-ounce can buttered lima beans
1 cup catsup
¼ cup brown sugar
3 tablespoons white vinegar
1 teaspoon salt
Black pepper to taste
1 tablespoon liquid smoke (optional)

Brown ground beef, bacon, and onion. Drain. Pour into baking dish or slow-cooker pot. Stir in remaining ingredients. Cook in baking dish in oven set at 325 degrees F. for 1½ hours, or in electric slow-cooker pot set on low for 4 to 6 hours. Makes 8 servings.

PORK TENDERLOIN

*3 to 4 pounds pork tenderloin (4
   tenderloins, each about 8 to 10
   inches long)*
3 to 4 cloves garlic, minced
½ cup soy sauce
½ cup sugar
¼ teaspoon monosodium glutamate
¼ to ½ teaspoon ginger
Red food coloring (optional)
*Chopped green onions and sesame
   seeds for garnish*

Place tenderloins in glass baking dish. Combine garlic, soy sauce, sugar, monosodium glutamate, ginger, and a drop or two of red food coloring; pour over meat. Cover with plastic wrap and refrigerate for several hours or overnight, turning a couple of times. Preheat oven to 325 degrees F. Cover meat and marinade with lid or aluminum foil and bake about 2 hours. When ready to serve, slice at an angle into serving pieces. Place on serving platter and pour marinade on top. Garnish with chopped green onions and sesame seeds. Makes 6 to 8 servings.

HOLIDAY OVEN OMELET

¼ cup margarine or butter
9 large eggs
1 cup sour cream
1 cup milk
2 teaspoons salt
¼ cup chopped chives or green onions
English Sausage Rolls (recipe below)

Preheat oven to 325 degrees F. Melt margarine in 9x13-inch baking dish. Beat eggs and add remaining ingredients. Pour into dish. Bake for 35 minutes or till eggs are done but still moist. Serve with English Sausage Rolls. Makes 8 to 10 servings.

ENGLISH SAUSAGE ROLLS

2 pounds bulk sausage
2 cups flour
½ teaspoon salt
4 teaspoons baking powder
1 tablespoon sugar
⅓ cup shortening

1 egg, beaten
½ cup milk

Preheat oven to 400 degrees F. Form sausage into 12 patties and brown lightly in fry pan. Drain and pat with paper towel to remove grease. Sift flour, salt, baking powder, and sugar in mixing bowl; cut in shortening. Add milk and egg and stir just enough to moisten. Roll out on slightly floured board. Cut squares of dough and wrap around each sausage patty. Place on greased baking sheet and bake for 15 minutes, or till pastry is golden brown. Serve with catsup or chili sauce. Makes 12 sausage rolls.

Variation: Use pie dough in place of shortcake dough.

VEGETARIAN QUICHE

1 10-inch pastry shell
4 cups cut-up fresh or frozen
*   vegetables (carrots, broccoli,*
*   cauliflower, zucchini, or Italian*
*   green beans)*
½ cup diced tomatoes
¼ cup chopped green onion
1½ cups grated Swiss cheese
4 eggs
1 cup half and half
½ cup sour cream
1 teaspoon salt
¼ teaspoon black pepper
¼ teaspoon oregano
½ teaspoon baking powder

Preheat oven to 400 degrees F. Bake pastry shell for 10 minutes. Remove from oven. Reset oven to 325 degrees F. Blanch vegetables in small amount of water till tender crisp. Drain and pour into bottom of pastry shell. Sprinkle with grated Swiss cheese. Beat together eggs, half and half, sour cream, salt, pepper, oregano, and baking powder. Pour over vegetables and cheese. Bake for 40 to 45 minutes. Makes 8 servings.

CRAB TETRAZZINI

8 ounces spaghetti, broken in pieces
3 to 4 inches long
2 cans (10½ ounces each) cream of
mushroom soup
1½ cups milk
5 tablespoons butter
¼ cup chopped green peppers
1 cup shredded Cheddar cheese
½ cup Parmesan cheese
1 pound imitation crabmeat

Cook broken spaghetti pieces in salted boiling water till done. Drain. Preheat oven to 350 degrees F. Mix soup, milk, butter, and green peppers together. Heat on stove or in microwave till butter is melted. Mix well. Add cooked spaghetti, Cheddar cheese, Parmesan cheese, and imitation crabmeat. Pour into 9x13-inch baking dish or large casserole dish. Cover with lid or aluminum foil. Bake till bubbly, for 30 to 40 minutes. If desired, sprinkle additional shredded cheese on top of casserole at the end of baking time. Makes 10 to 12 servings.

LEMON MARINATED SALMON

2 pounds salmon steaks or fillets
½ cup lemon juice
⅓ cup sliced green onion
¼ cup oil
3 tablespoons snipped parsley
3 tablespoons chopped green pepper
1 tablespoon sugar
2 teaspoons dry mustard
⅛ teaspoon cayenne or red pepper
½ teaspoon salt

Place fish on greased rack in fry pan. Pour in 1 cup water. Cover with a lid and steam for 5 to 7 minutes, or until fish is done and flakes easily when tested with a fork. Remove from pan to a shallow dish. In a screw-top jar, place the remaining ingredients. Shake vigorously to combine; pour over fish. Cover and chill several hours or overnight. Spoon marinade over fish several times. Drain before serving. Serve cold. Makes 6 servings.

HALIBUT BROIL AMANDINE

6 halibut steaks or fillets
1 cup chicken broth
2 tablespoons butter or margarine,
    melted
1 teaspoon dried thyme leaves
¼ cup butter or margarine
¼ cup sliced almonds
2 tablespoons lemon juice

Preheat broiler in oven. Rinse fish and pat dry. Arrange in a single layer in a greased baking pan. Pour broth around fish. Combine 2 tablespoons butter with thyme and brush part of it on fish. Place baking dish on broiler pan and put on oven rack about 3 to 4 inches from heat. Broil fish (do not turn), basting once or twice with remaining butter mixture: 3 to 6 minutes for fish ½- to ¾-inch thick or 6 to 10 minutes for fish 1- to 1¼-inches thick. Melt ¼ cup butter in small fry pan. Add almonds and stir till nuts begin to brown. Remove from heat and add lemon juice. Pour over fish when ready to serve. Makes 6 servings.

Variation: Use this cooking method for bass, cod, flounder, red snapper, shark, or orange roughy.

ORANGE ROUGHY WITH DILL

2 tablespoons butter or margarine
1 pound orange roughy fish fillets,
  thawed*
½ teaspoon dill weed
1 tablespoon lemon juice
Dash of salt and pepper
Buttered bread crumbs

Preheat oven to 450 degrees F. Melt butter in shallow baking dish. Place fish in melted butter, turning to coat; sprinkle with dill weed, lemon juice, and salt and pepper. Bake for 15 to 20 minutes, or till fish flakes easily with fork. Sprinkle lightly with buttered bread crumbs during last 3 minutes of baking. Makes 4 servings.

* Any white-fleshed, mild-flavored fish, such as haddock, sole, or whitefish, may be substituted for orange roughy.

BELL-RINGER
VEGETABLES

FESTIVE BEETS

1 16-ounce can diced beets
¼ cup sour cream
1 tablespoon tarragon or cider
  vinegar
1 teaspoon sugar
½ teaspoon salt
1 minced green onion
Dash cayenne

Heat beets; drain off liquid. Combine remaining ingredients; stir into beets.

Heat slowly. When hot, serve immediately. Makes 4 servings.

HOLIDAY CREAMED ONIONS

6 or 7 onions, peeled and sliced
1 cup water
⅔ cup milk
2 tablespoons butter
2 tablespoons flour
1 egg yolk, beaten
Salt and pepper to taste
Buttered bread crumbs
Slivered almonds

Combine sliced onions with water and cook till tender. Drain, saving liquid, and place onions in casserole dish. Mix onion liquid with milk in saucepan. Make roux by mixing butter and flour. Add roux to hot liquid and stir till thickened. Stir in beaten egg yolk and salt and pepper. Pour sauce over onions. Top with buttered bread crumbs and slivered almonds. Bake at 350 degrees F. till heated through. Makes 6 to 8 servings.

GLAZED BROCCOLI AMANDINE

2 pounds fresh broccoli (or 2 10-
 ounce packages frozen broccoli)
¼ cup butter or margarine
2 tablespoons flour
1 cup light cream
1 tablespoon lemon juice
¼ cup Parmesan cheese
¼ cup slivered almonds

Wash and separate broccoli into spears. Steam in a small amount of salted water till tender crisp. Drain. Make glaze by melting butter; add flour and stir into paste. Mix in cream and lemon juice and stir till thickened. Pour over broccoli. Sprinkle on Parmesan cheese and slivered almonds.

SPINACH SUPREME

2 10-ounce packages frozen chopped
 spinach
2 cups cooked rice
2 cups shredded Cheddar cheese
4 eggs, beaten
4 tablespoons soft margarine
⅔ cup milk
¼ cup chopped onion
1 tablespoon Worcestershire sauce
2 teaspoons salt
1 teaspoon crushed rosemary

Cook spinach and drain well. Combine rice with remaining ingredients. Stir in spinach. Pour mixture into greased casserole dish. Bake at 350 degrees F. for 35 minutes. Makes 8 servings.

NORTH POLE BROCCOLI

½ pound cooked broccoli
¾ cup mayonnaise
1 can (10½ ounces) cream of
   mushroom soup
⅔ cup evaporated milk
½ cup chopped onion
2 eggs, beaten
½ cup shredded Cheddar cheese
1 cup crushed round buttery crackers
¼ cup margarine, melted

Preheat oven to 350 degrees F. Coarsely chop broccoli. Mix mayonnaise and soup together; add evaporated milk and stir till blended. Add chopped onion, eggs, cheese, and broccoli. Pour into casserole dish. Mix cracker crumbs and margarine together and sprinkle on top of casserole. Bake for 20 to 30 minutes.

BROCCOLI VALHALLA

2 pounds fresh broccoli
3 large oranges
4 tablespoons margarine

Wash broccoli and cut into 2-inch pieces. Cook in a small amount of salted water till tender crisp. Drain. Peel and cut up oranges into chunks. Melt margarine and sauté oranges for a minute or two. Add broccoli and heat to blend flavors. Makes 6 servings.

CARAWAY CABBAGE

2 tablespoons butter or margarine
2 quarts shredded cabbage
1 clove garlic, pressed
¼ cup water
½ cup sour cream
1 tablespoon sugar
2 tablespoons vinegar
1 teaspoon salt
1 teaspoon caraway seeds

Heat butter in skillet. Add cabbage, garlic, and water; simmer about 5 minutes. Cover tightly and steam 10 to 12 minutes. Mix sour cream, sugar, vinegar, and salt and stir into cabbage. Heat thoroughly. Sprinkle with caraway seeds and serve immediately. Makes 6 servings.

ST. NICK'S GREEN BEANS

1½ pounds fresh green beans
1½ cups water
½ teaspoon salt
6 slices bacon
1 small onion, chopped
2 tablespoons flour
1 tablespoon vinegar
⅔ cup cream

Cook beans in boiling, salted water till tender. Fry bacon till crisp. Drain on paper towel and crumble. Using 2 tablespoons bacon drippings, sauté onion till clear. Add flour and stir to make roux; add vinegar. Stir this mixture into beans and liquid, and cook till thickened. Just before serving, stir in cream. Makes 6 servings.

HARVEST VEGETABLE BAKE

1 head cauliflower
½ cup chopped celery
⅓ cup chopped onion
⅓ cup chopped green pepper
3 tablespoons margarine
1 tablespoon cornstarch
1 cup milk
1 cup shredded Swiss cheese
¾ teaspoon salt
1 tomato, sliced
Paprika

Break cauliflower into flowerets and cook in small amount of salted water till tender. Drain and pour into shallow baking dish. In small saucepan, sauté celery, onion, and green pepper in melted margarine till tender crisp. Add to cauliflower. In same pan, mix cornstarch and cold milk and bring to boil, stirring till thickened. Stir in Swiss cheese and salt. Pour sauce over vegetables. Top with sliced tomato and sprinkle with paprika. Bake at 350 degrees F. 20 minutes. Makes 6 servings.

NUTMEG SPINACH SOUFFLÉ

1 pound fresh spinach
2 tablespoons margarine
2 tablespoons flour
1 teaspoon salt
1 cup milk
4 egg yolks, beaten
¼ cup chopped onion
⅛ teaspoon nutmeg
4 egg whites
¼ teaspoon cream of tartar
3 tablespoons Parmesan cheese

Wash spinach; cook in small amount of salted water. Drain and press out all excess water; chop spinach. Melt margarine in saucepan; add flour and salt and blend. Gradually add milk and stir till thickened. Gradually add beaten egg yolks. Stir in spinach, onion, and nutmeg. Beat egg whites and cream of tartar till stiff. Fold in spinach mixture. Pour into greased soufflé dish. Sprinkle with Parmesan cheese. Bake at 375 degrees F. for 50 minutes or till set. Makes 6 servings.

DELUXE PEAS AND CELERY

2 tablespoons butter
1 cup sliced mushrooms
½ cup celery, bias cut
2 tablespoons finely chopped onions
½ teaspoon salt
Black pepper to taste
¼ teaspoon savory salt
1 10-ounce package frozen peas,
    cooked and drained

Melt butter and sauté mushrooms, celery, and onions. Add salt, pepper, and savory salt. Mix in cooked peas. Makes 6 servings.

COMPANY CARROTS

2½ pounds carrots
¼ cup liquid from carrots
½ cup mayonnaise
1 tablespoon prepared horseradish
1 tablespoon minced parsley
Salt and pepper to taste
½ cup fine cracker crumbs
3 tablespoons margarine

Peel and cut carrots lengthwise into narrow strips. Cook in small amount of salted water till tender crisp. Drain carrots, saving ¼ cup liquid. Put carrots in 1½-quart casserole. Combine carrot liquid with mayonnaise, horseradish, parsley, salt, and pepper. Mix well and pour over carrots. Sprinkle cracker crumbs on top and dot with margarine. Bake, uncovered, at 375 degrees F. for 20 minutes. Makes 6 to 8 servings.

CARROTS LYONNAISE

6 medium carrots
1 chicken bouillon cube
½ cup boiling water
2 medium onions, sliced
2 tablespoons butter
1 tablespoon flour
¼ teaspoon salt
Dash of pepper
Pinch of sugar
¾ cup water

Pare carrots and cut in julienne strips. Dissolve bouillon cube in boiling water. Add carrots and cook for 7 to 10 minutes till tender crisp. While carrots are cooking, melt butter in small fry pan and add sliced onions. Cook and stir till clear. Add flour, salt, pepper, sugar, and ¾ cup water. Stir till thickened. Stir in carrots and chicken stock. Makes 6 servings.

SNOW-WHIPPED POTATO BOATS

6 large baking potatoes
3 slices bacon
½ cup sour cream
½ cup milk
1½ teaspoons salt
⅛ teaspoon pepper
4 chopped green onions
½ cup shredded Cheddar cheese

Preheat oven to 400 degrees F. Wash potatoes and rub skins with oil. Bake for 1 hour, or till potatoes are done. While potatoes are baking, cook bacon till crisp. Drain and crumble; set aside. Reduce oven heat to 350 degrees F. Cut a slice from top of each potato and scoop out pulp. Mash pulp; add sour cream, milk, salt, pepper, and green onions. Fill potato shells with mixture and sprinkle with shredded cheese and crumbled bacon. Bake at 350 degrees F. for 10 minutes. Makes 6 servings.

POTATOES AU GRATIN

6 medium potatoes
1 medium onion, chopped
½ green pepper, chopped fine
2 teaspoons salt
4 tablespoons margarine
½ cup flour
3½ cups milk
1¼ teaspoons salt
⅛ teaspoon black pepper
3 or 4 cups cubed cooked ham
1½ cups grated Cheddar cheese

Peel potatoes and cut into bite-size pieces. In saucepan, mix potatoes with onion, green pepper, and 2 teaspoons salt, and cover with water. Bring to boil. Turn off heat and let set for 5 minutes. Drain and spread potatoes in 9x13-inch baking pan. Make white sauce by melting margarine in saucepan. Stir in flour to make a paste. Add milk, 1¼ teaspoons salt, and pepper, and stir and cook till thickened. Mix in cubed ham and ¾ cup grated cheese. Pour over potatoes. Top with remaining cheese. Bake at 350 degrees F. for 35 to 40 minutes. Makes 10 to 12 servings.

ZUCCHINI BOATS

3 medium zucchini squash
1½ cups soft bread crumbs
¼ cup grated Parmesan cheese
1 egg, beaten
2 green onions, minced
1 tablespoon minced parsley
½ teaspoon salt
Paprika

Wash zucchini; cut off ends but don't peel. Cook in boiling, salted water for 7 to 10 minutes. Cut in half lengthwise; carefully remove pulp with spoon, leaving shell intact. Mash zucchini pulp with fork and mix with bread crumbs, Parmesan cheese, beaten egg, onions, parsley, and salt. Spoon mixture into shells and place in baking dish. Sprinkle with additional Parmesan cheese and paprika. Bake uncovered at 350 degrees F. for 30 minutes. Makes 6 servings.

LEMON PARSLEY TURNIPS

3 medium fresh turnips
1 tablespoon butter
2 teaspoons snipped parsley
1 teaspoon finely chopped green
  onion
1 teaspoon lemon juice

Peel and cut turnips into 2-inch strips, julienne style. Cook in small amount of salted water till tender, about 10 minutes. Drain. Add butter, parsley, onion, and lemon juice. Toss. Makes 6 servings.

ITALIAN ZUCCHINI BAKE

1½ pounds zucchini
2 tablespoons oil
1 cup sliced green onions
1 clove garlic, pressed
1½ cups stewed tomatoes
1 teaspoon garlic salt
½ teaspoon dry basil
½ teaspoon oregano leaves
½ teaspoon paprika
1 cup cooked rice
2 cups shredded sharp Cheddar
cheese

Cut zucchini into ¼-inch cubes (about 5 cups). In large fry pan, heat oil; stir in zucchini, onions, and garlic. Cover and cook for 5 minutes. Remove from heat and mix in tomatoes, garlic salt, basil, oregano, paprika, rice, and l cup of the cheese. Spoon mixture into a shallow 1½-quart baking dish and sprinkle with remaining 1 cup cheese. Bake, uncovered, at 350 degrees F. for 25 minutes. Makes 6 servings.

GRANDMA'S PARSNIP PUFFS

4 cups mashed cooked parsnips
1 cup flour
2 teaspoons baking powder
3 eggs, beaten
½ teaspoon salt
¼ teaspoon mace
Shortening for deep-fat frying

Peel and cut parsnips into 2-inch lengths, cutting out hard core if necessary. Place in saucepan with small amount of water and cook till tender, about 20 minutes. Drain and mash. Mix mashed parsnips with flour, baking powder, eggs, salt, and mace till well blended. Heat shortening in deep fryer to 375 degrees F. Drop parsnip batter by tablespoon into hot shortening and fry for 2 or 3 minutes till golden brown. Drain on paper towels. Makes 25 puffs.

PARSLEY RICE

1 cup uncooked rice
2 cups water
2 chicken bouillon cubes
2 tablespoons margarine
¼ cup minced green onion
⅓ cup diced green pepper
¼ cup slivered almonds
¼ cup chopped fresh parsley

Combine rice, water, and bouillon cubes in saucepan. Bring to boil. Reduce heat to low; cover and cook 15 minutes. Melt margarine and sauté onion, green pepper, and almonds for 1 minute. Mix into cooked rice, then fold in chopped parsley. Makes 6 servings.

CROOKNECK SQUASH SCALLOP

3 medium-size yellow crookneck
  squash
1 cup water
½ teaspoon salt
1 medium onion, sliced
¼ cup margarine
¼ cup flour
2½ cups milk
1 teaspoon salt
2 tablespoons chopped pimiento
1 cup cracker crumbs
3 tablespoons melted margarine

Wash and slice squash. Cook in boiling, salted water for 8 to 10 minutes. Add onions and continue cooking for another 5 minutes. Drain vegetables and put into casserole dish. Make white sauce by melting margarine; add flour, and stir to make roux. Slowly add milk and stir over medium heat till thickened. Stir in salt and pimiento. Pour sauce over squash. Mix cracker crumbs and margarine. Sprinkle on top of casserole. Bake at 350 degrees F. for 20 minutes. Makes 6 servings.

WHOLESOME
BREADS

HOLIDAY ALMOND TWISTS

1 tablespoon yeast
½ cup warm water
4½ cups flour
¼ cup sugar
1 teaspoon salt
1 teaspoon grated orange rind
1 cup butter, softened
6 eggs
ALMOND FILLING AND ICING
1 8-ounce can almond paste
½ cup butter, softened
¾ cup firmly packed brown sugar
¼ cup chopped almonds, toasted
2 cups sifted powdered sugar
3 tablespoons milk

Dissolve yeast in warm water in a large mixing bowl. Add 3 cups flour, sugar, salt, orange rind, butter, and eggs. Beat at low speed of electric mixer till blended. Beat 4 minutes at medium speed. Add remaining flour and continue beating at low speed till blended. Cover dough and let rise in warm place till doubled. Punch down; cover and refrigerate at least 8 hours.

Prepare Filling: Combine almond paste, butter, brown sugar, and chopped toasted almonds. Stir till blended. Punch dough down and divide in half. Place half on floured surface and roll to a 10x16-inch rectangle. Spread the dough with half the almond filling. Fold the dough lengthwise into thirds, forming a long rectangle. Cut rectangle into 16 1-inch strips. Twist each strip and place on greased baking sheet. Repeat with remaining dough and filling. Cover and let rise in a warm place till doubled. Bake at 350 degrees F. for 15 minutes or till golden brown. Remove from oven.

Prepare Icing: Combine powdered sugar and milk and drizzle over warm rolls. Makes 32 twists.

ENGLISH WIGS

2 tablespoons yeast
½ cup lukewarm water
½ cup sugar
½ cup margarine, melted
1¾ cups warm milk
1 egg, beaten
2 teaspoons salt
1½ teaspoons nutmeg
⅛ teaspoon cloves
⅛ teaspoon mace
6 to 7 cups flour
Beaten egg for tops of buns
Caraway seeds

Dissolve yeast in lukewarm water. Mix sugar, margarine, milk, beaten egg, salt, nutmeg, cloves, and mace. Add 3 cups of the flour and beat till smooth. Gradually add enough flour to make soft dough. Turn out onto floured surface and knead till smooth and elastic. Place in greased bowl; cover and let rise till dough doubles in bulk. Punch down. Divide dough in half. Form 12 round buns and place on greased baking sheet. Repeat with other half of dough. Cut a deep cross on each bun with sharp knife. Brush with beaten egg. Sprinkle with caraway seeds. Cover and let rise till doubled. Bake at 375 degrees F. for 20 minutes. Makes 24 buns.

Note: Serve these caraway-topped buns with hot spiced cider on Christmas Eve, or with raspberry jam as a Christmas-morning breakfast treat.

CURRANT-CREAM SCONES

1¾ cups flour
3 tablespoons sugar
2½ teaspoons baking powder
½ teaspoon salt
⅓ cup margarine
1 egg, beaten
½ cup currants
4 to 6 tablespoons light cream
Beaten egg for tops of scones

Combine flour, sugar, baking powder, and salt and cut margarine in until mixture resembles fine crumbs. Stir in beaten egg, currants, and just enough light cream so dough leaves side of bowl. Turn dough onto lightly floured surface. Knead lightly 10 times. Roll ½-inch thick. Cut dough with round biscuit cutter. Place on ungreased cookie sheet. Brush with beaten egg. Bake at 400 degrees F. until golden, 10 to 12 minutes. Serve hot with Whipped Honey-Orange Spread. Makes 10 to 12 scones.

WHIPPED HONEY-ORANGE SPREAD

In small bowl, beat 1 8-ounce package cream cheese, 2 tablespoons honey, and 1 tablespoon orange peel till light and fluffy. Store, covered, in refrigerator.

CHALLAH BRAID

1 tablespoon yeast
1½ cups lukewarm water
¼ cup sugar
¼ cup oil
1 teaspoon salt
2 eggs, well beaten
Pinch of saffron (optional)
4½ to 5 cups flour
1 egg yolk
Sesame seeds

Place yeast and water in large bowl. Add sugar, oil, salt, beaten eggs, saffron, and 2½ cups of the flour. Beat well. Add enough of the remaining flour to make soft dough; knead. Place in greased bowl. Cover and let rise till doubled in bulk. Punch down and divide into five pieces. Using four pieces, roll each into a long rope 18 to 20 inches long and one inch in diameter. Braid four ropes together. Cut remaining piece of dough into three pieces and roll each in a rope 8 inches long. Braid. Lay small braid on large braid. Place on cookie sheet. Brush with egg yolk mixed with ¼ teaspoon water. Sprinkle with sesame seeds. Cover and let rise 30 minutes. Bake at 375 degrees F. about 30 to 35 minutes. Makes one braid.

CRUNCHY ONION LOAF

1 tablespoon dry yeast
¼ cup lukewarm water
1 envelope onion soup mix
2 cups water
2 tablespoons sugar
1 teaspoon salt
2 tablespoons Parmesan cheese
2 tablespoons shortening
5 to 5½ cups flour
1 egg yolk, beaten
Cornmeal
1 egg white, beaten

Soften yeast in ¼ cup water. Mix soup mix and 2 cups water in saucepan and simmer 10 minutes. Add sugar, salt, Parmesan cheese, and shortening. Cool to lukewarm. Beat in 2 cups of the flour, egg yolk, and yeast. Add remaining flour a little at a time till dough is stiff enough to knead. Turn out on lightly floured surface and knead till smooth and elastic. Place in bowl, cover, and let rise till doubled in bulk. Punch down and divide in half. Shape into two round loaves. Place on greased baking sheet sprinkled with cornmeal. Cut several diagonal slashes in top and brush with slightly beaten egg white. Bake at 375 degrees F. for 30 minutes.

POTATO WHEAT BREAD

1 medium potato, cooked and mashed
2 cups potato water
1 tablespoon yeast
¼ cup lukewarm water
2 tablespoons honey
2 teaspoons salt
2 tablespoons oil
3 cups whole wheat flour
3 cups white flour

Peel and dice one medium potato and cover with about 3 cups water. Simmer till tender. Drain, saving 2 cups potato water. Mash potato. Dissolve yeast in ¼ cup lukewarm water. Add potato water, mashed potato, honey, salt, oil, and 2 cups of the whole wheat flour. Beat together for five minutes. Continue adding wheat and white flour till dough can be kneaded into a smooth ball. Cover and let rise till double in bulk. Punch down and knead again about 5 to 10 minutes. Cover and let rise again. Divide dough in half, and shape into loaves. Let rise 20 to 30 minutes. Bake at 375 degrees F. for 30 minutes. Makes 2 loaves.

CARAMEL-NUT BOW KNOTS

½ recipe Potato Wheat Bread dough
  (page 96)
¾ cup brown sugar
¼ cup white corn syrup
3 tablespoons margarine
2 teaspoons water
¾ cup chopped nuts
½ cup sugar
1 tablespoon cinnamon

Mix brown sugar, corn syrup, margarine, and water in saucepan. Heat till margarine is melted; simmer about 3 to 4 minutes. Spread in bottom of 9x13-inch baking dish. Sprinkle nuts on top of syrup mixture. Mix ½ cup sugar and the cinnamon together in a shallow dish. Pinch off a small amount of bread dough and roll between your hands till about 6 inches long. Tie in a knot. Dip the knot into the sugar-cinnamon mixture and place on top of syrup in pan. Repeat till pan is full of bow knots. Place pan in warm place to rise till double in bulk. Bake at 350 degrees F. for 20 to 25 minutes. Remove from oven and immediately turn over onto wax paper to let syrup drip down through the bow knots.

YULETIDE DANISH PASTRY

1 cup softened butter or margarine
2 cups warm milk
2 tablespoons yeast
1 tablespoon sugar
½ cup warm water
¾ cup sugar
1 teaspoon salt
2 eggs
8 cups flour
Cream Filling (recipe below)
Almond Filling (recipe below)
Streusel Topping (page 99)
Almond Icing (page 99)

Place all ingredients in large mixing bowl. Mix only till well blended. Cover and let rise till double. Punch down and roll out into desired shapes. In the meantime, make Cream and Almond fillings, Streusel topping, and Almond Icing.

Directions for Assembling: Divide dough into 4 equal parts. On lightly floured board, roll out each part into a rectangle. Spread ¼ Cream Filling on each; then ¼ Almond Filling on each. Roll up jelly-roll fashion. Cut about 10 slashes through top with knife. Place each roll on greased cookie sheet; then shape into wreath shape or candy cane shape. Sprinkle with Streusel Topping. Let rise in a warm place till double in bulk. Bake at 375 degrees F. for 20 minutes. Drizzle with Almond Icing and sprinkle with slivered or sliced almonds.

CREAM FILLING

1 cup milk
1 egg yolk
½ teaspoon salt
⅓ cup sugar
2 tablespoons flour

Heat milk in saucepan. Mix egg yolk into dry ingredients. Add a little warm milk, then mix with heated milk and stir and cook till thick. Cover with plastic wrap and cool.

ALMOND FILLING

½ cup butter or margarine
¾ cup sugar
½ cup oats
2 teaspoons almond flavoring

Mix all ingredients with fork or wire whip or mixer till well blended.

STREUSEL TOPPING

½ cup flour
½ cup sugar
½ cup butter

Mix all ingredients with fork or wire whip or mixer till well blended.

ALMOND ICING

1 cup powdered sugar
2 to 3 tablespoons milk or cream
1 teaspoon almond flavoring

Combine powdered sugar with enough milk or cream to make slightly runny icing. Add almond flavoring.

CRUSTY SOUP BOWLS

2 tablespoons yeast
2 cups warm water
1 tablespoon sugar
2 teaspoons salt
5 cups flour
Cornmeal

Dissolve yeast in water. Add sugar, salt, and 3 cups of the flour. Beat 3 minutes. Gradually add remaining flour to make stiff dough. Knead on lightly floured surface till dough is smooth and elastic. Place in greased bowl, cover, and let rise till double. Punch down, and divide into 8 pieces. Form each piece into ball and place on baking sheet sprinkled with cornmeal. Cover and let rise till double in bulk. Bake at 375 degrees F. for 25 minutes. Cool. Cut off tops; scoop out bread to make a bowl. Pour hot soup into bread bowl and serve. After soup is eaten, break off chunks of the crust and eat the bowl. Makes 8 large bread bowls.

GRANARY BREAD

1½ tablespoons yeast
3½ cups warm water
½ cup oil
½ cup honey
¼ cup molasses
1 tablespoon salt
1½ cups quick-cooking oats
1½ cups cracked wheat
½ cup wheat germ
½ cup soy flour
4½ cups whole wheat flour
2 cups white flour

Dissolve yeast in warm water. Add oil, honey, molasses, salt, oats, cracked wheat, wheat germ, and soy flour. Beat well. Gradually add whole wheat and white flours to form stiff dough. Knead till smooth and elastic. Place in greased bowl; cover and let rise till double in bulk. Punch down, divide in thirds, and mold into loaves. Place in greased loaf pans. Let rise till double. Bake at 350 degrees F. for 30 minutes. Makes 3 loaves.

PINWHEEL BREAD

WHITE DOUGH

3 cups warm water
2 tablespoons yeast
⅓ cup honey
⅓ cup oil
1 tablespoon salt
1 cup powdered milk
7 cups all-purpose flour

WHOLE WHEAT DOUGH

3 cups warm water
2 tablespoons yeast
⅓ cup honey
⅓ cup oil
1 tablespoon salt
1 cup powdered milk
7 cups whole wheat flour

To prepare white dough: Pour warm water into mixing bowl. Add yeast, honey, oil, salt, and milk. Add 3 cups of the flour and beat well. Add remaining flour 1 cup at a time till soft dough is formed. Knead on lightly floured board 7 minutes till smooth and elastic. Place in oiled bowl, cover, and let rise till double in bulk.

To prepare whole wheat dough: Follow directions for preparing white dough.

To form loaves: Divide doughs into equal portions. The number of loaves will depend on the size of pans used. Roll portion of white dough into a rectangle, then roll wheat dough into rectangle and place on top of white rectangle. Roll up like a jelly roll, sealing ends and bottom. Place in greased loaf pans. Let rise in warm place till double. Bake at 350 degrees F. for 35 minutes. Makes 6 loaves.

LION HOUSE PUMPKIN BREAD

1⅓ cups vegetable oil
5 eggs
1 16-ounce can pumpkin
2 cups flour
2 cups sugar
1 teaspoon salt
1 teaspoon cinnamon
1 teaspoon nutmeg
1 teaspoon baking soda
2 3-ounce packages vanilla pudding
*   mix (regular or instant)*
1 cup chopped nuts

Preheat oven to 350 degrees F. Mix oil, eggs, and pumpkin in mixing bowl and beat well. Sift together flour, sugar, salt, cinnamon, nutmeg, and baking soda. Add to pumpkin mixture and mix till blended. Stir in pudding mix and nuts. Pour into greased large loaf pans. Bake for 1 hour. Makes 2 loaves.

CRANBERRY NUT LOAF

2 cups flour
¾ cup sugar
1 teaspoon baking powder
½ teaspoon baking soda
1 teaspoon salt
¼ cup oil
1 egg, beaten
¾ cup orange juice
1 tablespoon grated orange peel
1 cup chopped fresh cranberries
½ cup chopped nuts

Preheat oven to 350 degrees F. Mix flour, sugar, baking powder, baking soda, and salt in mixing bowl. Add oil, egg, orange juice, and orange peel and stir just to moisten. Fold in cranberries and nuts. Grease bottom only of 1 large loaf pan or 2 small loaf pans. Pour batter into pan(s). Bake for 50 to 60 minutes. Cool slightly; loosen sides of loaf from pan and remove. Cool completely before slicing. Makes 1 large or 2 small loaves.

LEMON-GLAZED POPPY SEED BREAD

1¼ cups milk
⅓ cup oil
1 egg
1 teaspoon rum flavoring
2½ cups flour
1 cup sugar
¼ cup poppy seeds
3 teaspoons baking powder
1 teaspoon salt
½ cup powdered sugar
1 tablespoon lemon juice

Preheat oven to 350 degrees F. Mix milk, oil, egg, and rum flavoring together. In a separate mixing bowl, combine flour, sugar, poppy seeds, baking powder, and salt. Add liquid ingredients to dry ingredients and stir 30 seconds. Grease bottoms only of 1 large loaf pan or 2 small loaf pans. Pour batter into pan(s). Bake for 50 to 60 minutes. Loosen sides of loaf from pan; remove from pan. While still warm, drizzle with mixture of powdered sugar and lemon juice. Cool completely before slicing. Makes 1 large loaf or 2 small loaves.

ENGLISH BATTER BUNS

1 cup milk
½ cup shortening
2 tablespoons sugar
1 teaspoon salt
1½ tablespoons yeast
2 eggs, beaten
3½ cups flour

Heat milk. Add shortening, sugar, and salt. Cool to lukewarm and add yeast and eggs. Beat in flour. Cover and let rise till double in bulk. Stir down and spoon into greased muffin tins. Let rise again till double. Bake at 400 degrees F. for 10 minutes. Makes 12 large buns.

REFRIGERATOR ROLLS

1 cup shortening, melted
½ cup sugar
4 eggs
2½ cups water
2 tablespoons yeast
2 teaspoons salt
7 cups flour

Mix melted shortening, sugar, eggs, water, yeast, and salt with 3 cups of the flour. Gradually add rest of flour, 1 cup at a time, beating to make a soft dough. Place in 5-quart bowl. Cover tightly and refrigerate overnight. Two to three hours before baking, remove from refrigerator. Roll out on lightly floured surface. For Parkerhouse rolls, cut with biscuit cutter in circles; fold in half and place on greased cookie sheet. Allow to rise till double in bulk. Bake at 375 degrees F. for 15 minutes. Makes 4 dozen rolls.

Wheat Rolls: Use 4 cups whole wheat flour and 3 cups white flour.

LION HOUSE CRESCENT ROLLS

2 tablespoons yeast
2 cups warm water
⅓ cup sugar
⅓ cup shortening, margarine, or butter
2 teaspoons salt
⅔ cup nonfat dry milk
1 egg
5 to 6 cups flour
Melted butter or margarine

Mix yeast and water and let stand 5 minutes. Add sugar, shortening, salt, dry milk, egg, and 2 cups of the flour. Beat together till smooth. Gradually add remaining flour till soft dough is formed. Turn onto a lightly floured surface and knead till smooth and elastic. Place in greased bowl; cover and let rise till double in bulk. Punch down; divide into thirds. Roll out one-third of dough into circle; cut into 12 pie-shaped pieces. Starting at wide end, roll up each piece into crescent. Place on greased baking sheet with point on bottom. Repeat with remainder of dough. Brush tops with melted butter or margarine. Let rise till double. Bake at 400 degrees F. for 15 minutes. Serve warm with Honey Butter, if desired. Makes 3 dozen rolls.

HONEY BUTTER

½ cup softened butter
¼ teaspoon vanilla
1 egg yolk
1 cup honey

Whip butter. Add vanilla and egg yolk. Gradually whip in honey till light and fluffy.

HOT ORANGE ROLLS

1 tablespoon yeast
Pinch of sugar
¼ cup water
1 cup milk
1 tablespoon butter
½ cup sugar
½ teaspoon salt
3 eggs, beaten
4 cups flour
½ cup softened butter or margarine
½ cup sugar
Grated rind from 1 large orange

Dissolve yeast and pinch of sugar in ¼ cup water. Heat milk, butter, ½ cup sugar, and salt till butter is melted. Cool to lukewarm and beat in yeast mixture, eggs, and 1 cup of the flour. Let rise till bubbly. Gradually add remaining flour and beat well with spoon or mixer—not necessary to knead. Cover and let rise till double in bulk. Mix ½ cup softened butter, ½ cup sugar, and grated orange rind.

Roll dough out on lightly floured surface into rectangle and spread with sugar-orange mixture. (Save a little sugar mixture to sprinkle over rolls when done.) Roll up as for cinnamon rolls. Cut into slices and place in greased muffin tins. Let rise till double. Bake at 375 degrees F. for 15 to 20 minutes. Sprinkle with reserved sugar mixture. Makes 18 rolls.

OATMEAL APPLE MUFFINS

1 egg
1 cup flour
3 teaspoons baking powder
2 teaspoons cinnamon
1 teaspoon nutmeg
½ teaspoon salt
¾ cup milk
1 cup raisins
1 apple, peeled, cored, and chopped
½ cup vegetable oil
1 cup quick-cooking oats
⅓ cup brown sugar

Preheat oven to 400 degrees F. Beat egg. Sift together flour, baking powder, cinnamon, nutmeg, and salt. Combine all ingredients, mixing just to moisten. Spoon batter into greased muffin cups ¾ full. Bake for 15 to 20 minutes. Makes 12 muffins.

WHOLE WHEAT MUFFINS

1 cup whole wheat flour
1 cup white flour
½ cup brown sugar
½ teaspoon salt
4 teaspoons baking powder
⅓ cup melted shortening
2 eggs, beaten
1 cup milk
1 cup chopped walnuts

Preheat oven to 350 degrees F. Mix flours, brown sugar, salt, and baking powder in mixing bowl. Make a well and add melted shortening, eggs, and milk. Mix till just moistened. Fold in chopped nuts. Spoon into greased muffin cups ¾ full. Bake for 30 minutes. Makes 12 muffins.

GOLD-RUSH MUFFINS

3 eggs (or 6 egg whites)
⅓ cup brown sugar
½ cup vegetable oil
¼ cup molasses
2 cups unprocessed wheat bran
1 cup grated carrots
1 cup mashed bananas (2 large
* bananas)*
1½ cups apple juice or milk
1½ cups whole wheat flour
½ cup untoasted wheat germ
1 teaspoon baking soda
2 teaspoons baking powder
1 teaspoon salt
2 teaspoons cinnamon
½ cup raisins

Preheat oven to 375 degrees F. In large bowl, beat eggs. Add brown sugar, oil, molasses, bran, carrots, banana, and apple juice or milk; stir well. In separate bowl, mix whole wheat flour, wheat germ, baking soda, baking powder, salt, and cinnamon; stir in raisins, then add all at once to egg mixture, stirring only till moistened. Spoon into muffin cups ¾ full. Bake for 25 minutes. Makes 2 dozen muffins.

CREPES

3 eggs
½ cup milk
½ cup water
3 tablespoons butter, melted
¾ cup flour
½ teaspoon salt

Combine all ingredients in blender container; blend about 1 minute. Scrape down sides with rubber spatula, and blend about 30 seconds more. Refrigerate for 1 hour. To cook, heat omelet, crepe, or regular frying pan on medium-high heat just hot enough to sizzle a drop of water. Brush lightly with melted butter. For each crepe, pour in just enough butter to cover bottom of pan, tipping and tilting pan to move batter quickly over bottom. If crepe has holes, add a drop or two of batter to patch. Cook till light brown on bottom and dry on top. Remove from pan and stack on plate. Makes 12 crepes.

LORENZO SNOW'S YORKSHIRE PUDDING

1 egg
1 cup milk
½ cup flour
Pinch of salt
Dripping from roast beef

Preheat oven to 425 degrees F. Beat egg lightly and add milk. Sift flour and salt. Gradually add egg and milk mixture, stirring carefully to prevent lumps. Put about 1 teaspoon drippings from roast in each cup of muffin tin. Place muffin tins in very hot oven till sizzling. Reduce heat of oven to 350 degrees F. Fill each cup of muffin tin half full with batter. Bake 15 minutes. Makes 8 to 10 servings.

(Source: Salt Lake 18th Ward Cookbook)

YULETIDE DESSERTS

STEAMED CARROT PUDDING

1¾ cups flour
1½ cups sugar
1½ teaspoons baking soda
½ teaspoon salt
1 teaspoon cinnamon
¾ teaspoon nutmeg
¼ teaspoon cloves
1½ cups grated carrots
1½ cups grated potatoes
¼ cup melted butter or margarine
1 cup coarsely chopped nuts
Butterscotch Sauce (recipe below)

Mix all ingredients together in large mixing bowl till well blended. Pour into 8-cup greased pudding mold or divide into 2 or 3 cans, filling ⅔ full. Cover with foil. Place on rack in pan with 2 inches of water. Cover pan, and steam on low heat on top of stove for 2 hours. Check water level occasionally and add more, if necessary. Serve warm with Butterscotch Sauce. Makes 8 to 10 servings.

To flame pudding: Soak sugar cubes in lemon extract. Just before serving, place cube on top of pudding and light.

BUTTERSCOTCH SAUCE

1½ cups brown sugar
⅔ cup light corn syrup
½ cup water
Dash of salt
⅔ cup evaporated milk

Combine brown sugar, corn syrup, water, and salt in small saucepan. Heat to boiling, stirring till sugar is dissolved. Continue cooking till a small amount forms a very soft ball in cold water. Remove from heat. Cool slightly, then stir in evaporated milk. Makes 2 cups sauce.

HEBER J. GRANT'S
CHRISTMAS FIG PUDDING

2 pounds white dried figs
8 cups soft bread crumbs
4 cups brown sugar
1 cup white sugar
1 pound ground suet
3 tablespoons molasses
4 tablespoons flour
3 teaspoons grated nutmeg
Juice of 4 lemons
8 eggs

Grind figs in meat grinder. Mix with all other ingredients except eggs. Beat egg yolks and egg whites separately. Stir yolks into fig mixture, then fold in whites. Thoroughly grease five 1-pound cans and fill ⅔ full. Steam for 3 hours. If pudding is made ahead, let cool completely and then refrigerate.

(Source: Frances Grant Bennett, daughter of President Heber J. Grant)

SPENCER W. KIMBALL'S RASPBERRY CHEESECAKE

1 3-ounce package lemon gelatin
1 cup hot water
1 cup evaporated milk, chilled and
  whipped
1 8-ounce package cream cheese,
  softened
1 cup sugar
2 teaspoons lemon juice
½ cup butter
28 graham crackers, crushed
1 cup whipping cream, whipped and
  sweetened
1 to 2 cups fresh or frozen
  raspberries

Dissolve gelatin in hot water; cool and blend in whipped evaporated milk. Beat cream cheese with sugar. Gently combine gelatin mixture and cream cheese and fold in lemon juice. Melt butter and combine with cracker crumbs. Place half of crumbs on bottom of 9x13-inch pan. Pour gelatin/ cream cheese mixture on top and sprinkle with remaining crumbs. Chill at least 3 hours to set. Serve with whipped cream and fresh or frozen raspberries. Makes 10 to 12 servings.

(Source: Olive Kimball Mack, daughter of President Spencer W. Kimball)

LION HOUSE CHEESECAKE

1½ cups graham cracker crumbs,
  rolled fine
3 tablespoons butter or margarine
1 teaspoon cinnamon
3 8-ounce packages cream cheese,
  softened
1 cup sugar
3 eggs
¾ teaspoon vanilla
1 pint sour cream
3 tablespoons sugar
½ teaspoon vanilla

Preheat oven to 350 degrees F. Mix graham cracker crumbs, butter, and cinnamon. Press firmly into bottom and sides of a 9- or 10-inch springform pan. Whip cream cheese; gradually add sugar; then add eggs one at a time. Stir in vanilla. Pour filling into crust. Bake 40 minutes. Whip sour cream; add sugar and vanilla. Spread on top of cheesecake and return to oven. Bake for 10 minutes more. Cool before removing sides from pan. Refrigerate till ready to serve. Makes 10 to 12 servings.

CHEESECAKE FOR A CROWD

1 package white cake mix
2 8-ounce packages cream cheese,
  softened at room temperature
4 cups powdered sugar
1 pint whipping cream, whipped
2 16-ounce cans cherry, raspberry, or
  strawberry pie filling

Preheat oven to 350 degrees F. Grease and flour two 9x13-inch baking pans. Prepare cake according to package directions, and pour half of cake batter in each pan. Bake for 20 minutes or until cake tests done. Remove from oven and cool. Whip cream cheese and powdered sugar together till fluffy. Add whipped cream. Spread mixture onto both cakes. Spread pie filling on top of cream cheese layer. Refrigerate till ready to serve. Makes 24 to 30 servings.

Variation: Instead of pie filling, substitute Danish Dessert prepared according to package directions, and stir in drained fruit of your choice.

DAVID O. MCKAY'S BAKED APPLES

6 apples
¾ cup brown, white, or maple sugar
Lemon juice
Cinnamon
Butter
Cream

Preheat oven to 375 degrees F. Wash and core apples. Fill center of each apple with 1 tablespoon sugar, sprinkling a little over the outside. Then sprinkle with lemon juice and cinnamon, and dot with butter. Place in deep casserole with a lid. Add enough water to cover bottom of baking dish. Cover and bake about 35 minutes or till tender. Remove apples and boil syrup remaining in the casserole dish till thick. Pour syrup and thick cream over apples to serve. (If apples are baked uncovered, it is necessary to baste them during cooking.) Makes 6 servings.

(Source: Emma Rae McKay Ashton, daughter of President David O. McKay.)

CHRISTMAS RASPBERRY CRUNCH

2 cups crushed pretzels
3 tablespoons sugar
½ cup margarine or butter
1 8-ounce package cream cheese,
  softened
1 cup sugar
1 12-ounce carton whipped topping
1 16-ounce can crushed pineapple,
  drained
1 6-ounce package raspberry gelatin
3 cups boiling water
1 10-ounce package frozen raspberries

Preheat oven to 400 degrees F. Crush pretzels with rolling pin. Mix with sugar and melted butter. Press into bottom of 9x13-inch baking pan. Bake 5 minutes. Cool. Beat cream cheese and sugar till fluffy. Mix in whipped topping. Fold in drained pineapple. Spread mixture onto cooled pretzel crust. Dissolve gelatin in boiling water. Mix in frozen raspberries. Place gelatin in refrigerator till syrupy. Pour over cream cheese layer. Refrigerate till set. Garnish with whipped cream. Makes 12 servings.

CHOCOLATE-PEPPERMINT DELIGHT

2 cups crushed vanilla wafers
¼ cup margarine, melted
½ cup butter
1½ cups powdered sugar
3 eggs
2 squares unsweetened chocolate,
  melted
1 cup whipping cream
8 ounces miniature marshmallows
½ cup crushed peppermint candy

Mix vanilla wafers with melted margarine and press into an 8x8-inch pan. Cream butter and powdered sugar till fluffy. Add eggs and continue to beat; slowly add chocolate. Spread mixture on top of vanilla wafers; chill. Whip cream till stiff and combine with marshmallows. Spread over chocolate layer. Sprinkle crushed peppermint candy on top. Refrigerate several hours before serving. Makes 9 servings.

ALMOND RICE PUDDING

½ cup uncooked rice
2 cups milk
1 envelope unflavored gelatin
¼ cup cold water
¼ cup blanched almonds, chopped
1 teaspoon vanilla
5 tablespoons sugar
Dash of salt
2 cups whipping cream, whipped
Fruit sauce

Bring milk to a boil. Add rice and reduce heat. Simmer, covered, till done, about 20 to 25 minutes. Dissolve gelatin in water. Stir into rice the gelatin, chopped almonds, vanilla, sugar, and salt. Cool slightly. Fold in whipped cream. Pour into bowl. Refrigerate. Serve with cold fruit sauce, such as cherry sauce or Danish Dessert made according to package directions. Makes 8 servings.

JOSEPH FIELDING SMITH'S
FAVORITE SHERBET

5 cups sugar
1 teaspoon salt
3 tablespoons cornstarch
2 quarts water
1 quart whipping cream
2 quarts milk
Juice of 6 oranges
Juice of 2 lemons
1 16-ounce can crushed pineapple
* and juice*
3 or 4 bananas, mashed

Combine sugar, salt, cornstarch, and water. Cook till clear, then cool. Add whipping cream and milk. Add orange juice and lemon juice, crushed pineapple, and mashed bananas. Pour into 8-quart ice cream freezer and freeze. (Cut recipe in half to make 4 quarts.)

(Source: Amelia Smith McConkie, daughter of President Joseph Fielding Smith)

HARVEST PEACH ICE CREAM

8 large fresh peaches
Juice of 2 lemons
3 cups sugar
1 14-ounce sweetened condensed milk
2 cups whipping cream, whipped
1 quart milk

Peel and mash peaches. Mix with lemon juice and sugar and let stand in refrigerator for two hours. Mix peach mixture with sweetened condensed milk, whipped cream, and milk. Pour into 4-quart ice cream freezer can. Freeze according to freezer directions. Makes 4 quarts.

FROSTY VANILLA ICE CREAM

4 junket tablets
¼ cup cold water
2 quarts milk
2 cups whipping cream
2 cups sugar
⅛ teaspoon salt
4 teaspoons vanilla

Dissolve junket tablets in cold water. Mix milk, cream, sugar, and salt, and heat to lukewarm. Add dissolved junket tablets and vanilla. Pour into freezer can. Put dasher in place and let stand 10 minutes to set. Then freeze according to freezer directions. Makes 4 quarts.

Variations: Add 2 cups mashed fresh or frozen thawed fruit, such as raspberries, strawberries, peaches, or boysenberries.

PANTRY LEMON KRACKLE

1½ cups brown sugar
1½ cups flour
20 soda crackers, crushed
¾ teaspoon baking soda
1 cup margarine, softened
¾ cup chopped nuts
Juice of 4 lemons
4 eggs, beaten
2 cups water
2 cups sugar
¼ cup cornstarch
¼ cup margarine
1 teaspoon vanilla
Whipped cream
Lemon slices for garnish

Mix brown sugar, flour, crushed crackers, and baking soda. Cut in 1 cup margarine till crumbly. Stir in nuts. Press mixture into bottom of 9x13-inch baking pan. Make filling by mixing lemon juice, beaten eggs, and water in saucepan. Mix 2 cups sugar with cornstarch and add to liquid. Cook and stir till thickened. Stir in ¼ cup margarine and vanilla. Pour filling on top of crust. Bake for 30 minutes at 350 degrees F. Serve with whipped cream and garnish with lemon slice. Makes 12 servings.

PISTACHIO PUDDING

2 cups biscuit mix
2 tablespoons brown sugar
¼ cup margarine
½ cup chopped nuts
1½ cups powdered sugar
2 8-ounce packages cream cheese,
    softened
½ pint whipping cream, whipped
1 quart milk
2 packages (3½ ounces each)
    pistachio instant pudding
Whipped cream and green cherries
    for garnish

Preheat oven to 375 degrees F. Combine biscuit mix and brown sugar, and cut in margarine till crumbly. Add chopped nuts. Press into a 9x13-inch baking pan. Bake 10 minutes. Cool. Cream powdered sugar and cream cheese till fluffy. Fold in whipped cream. Spread mixture over baked crust. Pour milk into bowl. Add pudding mix and beat till well blended. Pour over cream cheese layer. Refrigerate. Garnish with whipped cream and green cherry. Makes 12 to 15 servings.

WINTER PEARS WITH RASPBERRY SAUCE

1 3-ounce package cream cheese,
  softened
¼ cup ricotta cheese
2 tablespoons finely chopped pecans
4 fresh medium pears
1½ cups fresh or frozen raspberries
3 tablespoons water
1 tablespoon sugar
1 teaspoon cornstarch

Combine softened cream cheese, ricotta cheese, and pecans. Wash pears; pat dry. Core each of the pears, leaving a center hole about 1 inch in diameter. Fill each pear center with the cream cheese-nut mixture. Chill. Make sauce by pressing raspberries through a sieve to remove seeds. Combine raspberries and juice with water, sugar, and cornstarch. Cook and stir till thickened. Chill. To serve, cut pears crosswise into ¼-inch slices. For each serving, spoon a little sauce onto dessert plate, and place 4 or 5 pear slices on top of sauce. Makes 6 servings.

BUCHE DE NOEL (Yule Log)

CAKE ROLL
3 eggs
1 cup sugar
⅓ cup water
1 teaspoon vanilla
¾ cup flour
¼ cup cocoa
1 teaspoon baking powder
¼ teaspoon salt
Powdered sugar

Preheat oven to 375 degrees F. Line a jelly-roll pan (10x15-inch pan) with wax paper; grease paper.

Prepare cake roll: Beat eggs in mixer bowl on high speed till thick and lemon colored, about 5 minutes. Gradually beat in 1 cup sugar. Beat in water and 1 teaspoon vanilla on low speed. Sift together flour, ¼ cup cocoa, baking powder, and salt; add to egg and sugar mixture, beating just till batter is smooth. Pour into jelly roll pan. Bake for 15 minutes. Cool 5 minutes. Turn out onto a dish towel sprinkled with powdered sugar. Remove wax paper and roll cake and towel from short end; cool.

FILLING
1 cup whipping cream
2 tablespoons sugar

FROSTING
⅓ cup cocoa
⅓ cup margarine, softened
2 cups powdered sugar
1½ teaspoons vanilla
1 to 2 tablespoons hot water
Green and red candied cherries

Prepare filling: Beat whipping cream till stiff. Add sugar. Unroll cake, and spread whipped cream over cake. Roll up again and place seam-side down on serving plate.

Prepare frosting: Mix cocoa, margarine, 2 cups powdered sugar, and vanilla. Add hot water till smooth and of spreading consistency. Cover roll with frosting, making strokes with tines of fork to resemble bark. Decorate with green and red candied cherries. Refrigerate till ready to serve. Makes 10 to 12 servings.

FROSTY FRAPPE FOR A CROWD

1 gallon pineapple sherbet
3 10-ounce packages frozen
   raspberries
1½ cups frozen blueberries
1½ cups frozen boysenberries
4 or 5 bananas, peeled and mashed
½ to 1 large (2-liter) bottle lemon-
   lime soda

Soften sherbet and partially thaw raspberries, blueberries, and boysenberries. Spoon sherbet into large bowl. Add partially thawed fruits and mashed bananas and stir just till blended. Stir in carbonated lemon-lime beverage a little at a time to keep slushy consistency. Serve immediately by spooning into punch cups. Makes 32 servings.

ENGLISH TRIFLE

2 to 3 cups stale sponge cake or
  vanilla wafers
1 16-ounce can fruit cocktail (or any
  kind of fruit)
1 3-ounce package gelatin
  (strawberry, raspberry, or cherry)
1 3-ounce package instant vanilla
  pudding*
2 cups cold milk
2 cups whipping cream
Chopped nuts
Grated chocolate
Maraschino cherries

Line bottom of glass serving bowl with pieces of sponge cake or vanilla wafers. Drain fruit and arrange over cake. Make gelatin according to package directions, and while still warm, pour over the cake and fruit. Allow to set. Make vanilla pudding by beating pudding powder into cold milk. Pour over set gelatin. Cover with plastic wrap and refrigerate. When ready to serve, whip cream and spread over top of pudding. Decorate with chopped nuts, grated chocolate, and maraschino cherries. Makes 8 to 10 servings.

For a true English trifle, use Bird's Custard powder, which is available at many food stores in gourmet or imported-foods section. Prepare according to directions on package.

ZINA'S CARAMEL DUMPLINGS

2 tablespoons butter
1½ cups brown sugar
1½ cups water
1¼ cups flour
½ cup sugar
2 teaspoons baking powder
½ teaspoon salt
½ cup milk
1 teaspoon vanilla

To make caramel sauce, combine butter, brown sugar, and water in saucepan. Bring to boil; reduce heat to simmer. Make dumplings by mixing flour, sugar, baking powder, and salt in bowl; stir in milk and vanilla (batter should be stiff). Drop by teaspoon into simmering caramel sauce. Cover pan and simmer for 20 minutes. Do not remove lid till time is up. Spoon into serving dishes and serve with cream or ice cream, if desired. Makes 6 servings.

RAISIN CREAM PIE

1 cup seedless raisins
1½ cups water
¾ cup sugar
3 tablespoons cornstarch
¼ teaspoon salt
1 teaspoon vanilla
1 tablespoon butter
1 cup light cream
Pastry for 9-inch 2-crust pie

Rinse and drain raisins. Put in saucepan, add water, and boil slowly 10 minutes. Blend sugar, cornstarch, and salt. Add to raisin mixture and cook, stirring constantly, till clear and thick. Remove from heat and stir in vanilla, butter, and cream. Pour into pastry-lined pie pan and cover with pastry. Bake at 400 degrees F. for 30 minutes or till pastry is light brown. Serve warm or cold. Makes 6 to 8 servings.

CRANBERRY PIE

2½ *cups fresh cranberries*
1 *cup water*
¾ *cup raisins*
1 *cup sugar*
4 *tablespoons cornstarch*
½ *cup chopped walnuts*
2 *tablespoons butter*
Baked 9-inch pie shell
Whipped cream

In a medium saucepan cook cranberries in 1 cup water till cranberries pop. Add raisins. Combine sugar and cornstarch and stir into cranberry mixture. Cook and stir till mixture thickens and bubbles. Add nuts and butter and stir till butter melts. Pour into pie shell. Cool. Serve with a dollop of whipped cream. Makes 6 to 8 servings.

JOSEPH F. SMITH'S CUSTARD PIE

2 *cups milk*
4 *eggs*
½ *cup sugar*
Pinch of salt
Generous sprinkling of nutmeg
1 *unbaked 9-inch pie shell*

Preheat oven to 375 degrees F. Put milk in bowl. Beat eggs and strain through fine sieve into bowl of milk. Add sugar, salt, and nutmeg. Stir well and pour into pie shell. Bake till knife just barely comes out clean, about 50 to 60 minutes. Do not overcook, or custard will become watery. Makes 6 to 8 servings. *Note:* This recipe calls for no vanilla.

(Source: Salt Lake City 18th Ward Cookbook)

EZRA TAFT BENSON'S
LEMON MERINGUE PIE

Grated rind from 2 lemons
3 cups sugar
2 heaping tablespoons flour
2 heaping tablespoons cornstarch
5 egg yolks, well-beaten
4 cups water
Juice of 2 lemons
1 tablespoon butter
1 9-inch baked pie shell

MERINGUE
5 egg whites
3 tablespoons sugar

Grate outside rind of two lemons; add sugar, flour, and cornstarch. Stir in beaten egg yolks, then water and lemon juice. Over medium heat, stir constantly till the mixture is thickened. Stir in butter. Pour into pie shell.

Prepare Meringue: Beat egg whites until foamy; stir in 3 tablespoons sugar and continue beating until stiff. Carefully spoon onto pie. Bake at 425 to 450 degrees F. for 3 to 5 minutes, or till meringue is lightly browned.

(Source: Flora Amussen Benson, wife of President Ezra Taft Benson)

LEMON CHIFFON PIE

1¼ cups graham cracker crumbs
⅓ cup melted butter
¼ cup sugar
1 envelope unflavored gelatin
½ cup sugar
⅛ teaspoon salt
4 egg yolks, beaten
½ cup cold water
1 teaspoon grated lemon peel
½ cup lemon juice
4 egg whites
½ cup sugar

Preheat oven to 375 degrees F. Make crust by mixing graham cracker crumbs, melted margarine, and ¼ cup sugar. Press mixture evenly in bottom and up sides of 9-inch pie pan. Bake for 8 minutes. Cool. Make filling by combining gelatin, ½ cup sugar, and salt in saucepan. Stir in beaten egg yolks, water, lemon peel, and lemon juice. Cook and stir over medium heat till gelatin dissolves and mixture is thick and bubbly. Remove from heat. Chill to consistency of corn syrup, stirring occasionally. Beat egg whites till soft peaks form. Gradually add ½ cup sugar, beating till stiff peaks form. Fold egg whites into lemon mixture. Spoon into graham cracker shell. Chill for several hours before serving. Serve with dollop of whipped cream and garnish with thin lemon slice. Makes 6 to 8 servings.

CHOCOLATE ANGEL PIE

2 egg whites (room temperature)
⅛ teaspoon salt
⅛ teaspoon cream of tartar
½ cup sugar
½ cup finely chopped nuts
½ teaspoon vanilla
1 8-ounce milk chocolate bar with
   almonds
1½ cups heavy cream, whipped
1 teaspoon vanilla

Preheat oven to 300 degrees F. Beat egg whites, salt, and cream of tartar till frothy. Add sugar gradually, beating till stiff peaks form. Fold in nuts and vanilla. Spread into greased 9-inch pie pan, building up on sides of pie pan. Bake for 50 minutes. Cool completely. Break up ¾ of chocolate bar into pieces and melt in top of double boiler or microwave in glass bowl. When chocolate is just lukewarm, fold into whipped cream and vanilla. Pile chocolate filling into cooled meringue shell. Grate remaining chocolate to garnish pie. Chill in refrigerator for two hours before serving. Makes 6 to 8 servings.

UNBAKED DATE-NUT ROLL

½ pound graham crackers
½ pound miniature marshmallows
½ cup nuts, chopped
½ pound dates, cut in small pieces
1 cup cream
Whipped cream to garnish

Crush graham crackers with rolling pin; set aside about ¼ of the crumbs. Mix marshmallows, nuts, and dates with remaining ¾ of graham cracker crumbs. Add cream to moisten. Mold into a long roll; then roll in reserved crumbs. Wrap in wax paper and refrigerate. When ready to serve, slice and garnish with whipped cream. Makes 8 servings.

NORTH POLE TOFFEE CAKE

1 20-ounce package chocolate cake
  mix
1 12-ounce carton frozen whipped
  topping
⅓ cup chocolate syrup
7 toffee bars (Heath or Skor), crushed

Grease and flour two 9-inch round cake pans. Prepare and bake cake according to package directions. Cool on wire rack. Carefully cut each layer horizontally to make 2 layers. In a bowl mix whipped topping with chocolate syrup and 6 crushed toffee bars. Place 1 layer of cake on serving plate and spread with chocolate mixture. Repeat with remaining 3 layers. Frost sides and top of cake. Sprinkle remaining crushed bar on top of cake.

CHRISTMAS ANGEL CAKE

1 10-inch angel food cake, baked and
  cooled
1 10-ounce package frozen
  strawberries, thawed
1 envelope unflavored gelatin
2 cups heavy cream, whipped till stiff
4 tablespoons sugar
1 teaspoon almond flavoring
Fresh strawberries for garnish

Cut angel food cake into 3 horizontal layers. Drain juice off thawed strawberries into small bowl. Sprinkle gelatin into juice to soften; set small bowl into hot water and stir till gelatin dissolves. Combine the gelatin mixture with berries. Whip cream; add sugar and almond flavoring. Fold strawberries into whipped cream. Spread whipped cream between layers and on top and sides of cake. Decorate with whole strawberries. Refrigerate till firm. Makes 10 to 12 servings.

DANISH ALMOND GIFT CAKE

1¾ cups plus 2 tablespoons margarine
2½ cups sugar
4 eggs
2½ cups plus 2 tablespoons sifted flour
1 teaspoon baking powder
½ cup warm water
4 teaspoons almond extract
1 cup sliced almonds
Pearl sugar*

Preheat oven to 375 degrees F. Grease well two 9-inch or three 8-inch round cake pans. Cream margarine and sugar till fluffy. Beat in eggs one at a time till light and fluffy, about 7 to 10 minutes. Sift flour and baking powder, and add to creamed mixture alternately with water and almond extract. Pour batter into baking pans, and sprinkle tops with sliced almonds and pearl sugar. Bake 30 to 35 minutes or until cake tests done. Remove from oven and invert on wire rack to cool. Store in covered cake container or cover with foil or plastic wrap.

*Pearl sugar is available in the gourmet section of grocery stores.

LIGHT FRUIT CAKE

1 pound flaked coconut
½ pound red candied pineapple
½ pound green candied pineapple
1 pound red candied cherries
1 pound green candied cherries
1 pound whole Brazil nuts
1 pound pecan halves
¾ cup flour
2 cans sweetened condensed milk

Preheat oven to 250 degrees F. Line six 4½x8½-inch loaf pans with greased wax paper. Mix coconut, candied fruits, and nuts in large mixing bowl. Add flour and mix well. Add sweetened condensed milk and stir till blended. Divide batter into pans. Bake for 2½ hours, or till wooden pick inserted in center comes out clean. Remove from pans and cool on wire rack. Wrap in plastic wrap or aluminum foil. Store in refrigerator 3 to 4 weeks or freeze. Makes six small loaves.

GLAZED PRUNE CAKE

2 cups sugar
1 cup vegetable oil
4 eggs
1 teaspoon baking soda
1 cup buttermilk
2½ cups flour
½ teaspoon salt
1 teaspoon cinnamon
1 teaspoon cloves
1 cup chopped cooked prunes
1 cup chopped nuts

GLAZE
1 cup sugar
½ cup butter, softened
½ cup buttermilk
1 teaspoon baking soda
1 tablespoon corn syrup
½ teaspoon vanilla

Preheat oven to 350 degrees F. Grease a 9x13-inch pan. Combine sugar, oil, and eggs and beat till light. Mix baking soda with buttermilk. Sift flour, salt, cinnamon, and cloves. To creamed mixture, add buttermilk mixture alternately with sifted dry ingredients. Stir in prunes and nuts. Pour into greased pan. Bake for 1 hour or until cake tests done. While cake is baking, prepare glaze by mixing in a saucepan the sugar, butter, ½ cup buttermilk, 1 teaspoon baking soda, and corn syrup. Cook over medium heat for 10 minutes, stirring occasionally. Remove from heat and stir in vanilla. When cake is done, remove from oven and pour glaze over top of hot cake. Cool cake before cutting.

Variation: Add 1 cup chocolate chips to cake batter.

HAROLD B. LEE'S FRUIT CAKE

1 pound butter, softened
2 cups sugar
6 eggs, beaten
1 teaspoon baking soda
2 cups sour milk or buttermilk
5 cups flour
1 teaspoon salt
1 teaspoon baking powder
1 teaspoon each: cinnamon, cloves,
*   allspice, nutmeg*
½ cup sugar
⅓ cup boiling water
Juice and grated rind of 1 lemon
Juice and grated rind of 1 orange
2 pounds seeded raisins
1 pound currants
1 pound walnuts
½ pound fruit-flavored gumdrops,
*   cut into small pieces*

Cream softened butter and sugar together. Add beaten eggs. Add soda to sour milk. Sift together flour, salt, baking powder, and spices, and add alternately with milk and soda. Melt sugar in heavy pan over low heat, stirring constantly; heat until melted to a golden brown syrup. Add boiling water to hot caramelized sugar and stir quickly. Add this mixture to batter and mix thoroughly. Add lemon and orange juice. Mix together grated rind, raisins, currants, walnuts, and gumdrops and stir into batter. Divide batter into greased loaf tins that have been lined with brown paper. Bake at 275 degrees F. for three hours. Cool. Store in tightly covered container for 2 to 3 weeks to ripen.

(Source: Helen Lee Goates, daughter of President Harold B. Lee)

PARADISE CAKE

1 can (11½ ounces) mandarin
  oranges
4 eggs
½ cup vegetable oil
1 package yellow pudding cake mix
1 20-ounce can crushed pineapple
  with juice
1 3-ounce package vanilla instant
  pudding
1 8-ounce carton frozen whipped
  topping, thawed

Preheat oven to 350 degrees F. Grease 9x13-inch baking pan. Combine mandarin oranges and juice, eggs, and oil in mixing bowl; beat well. Stir in cake mix and beat again till well mixed. Pour into greased baking pan. Bake for 30 minutes or till cake tests done.

Leave cake in pan to cool. Make topping by mixing crushed pineapple and juice, vanilla instant pudding, and whipped topping. Spread onto cooled cake in pan. Refrigerate till ready to serve.

PINEAPPLE UPSIDE-DOWN CAKE

¼ cup butter or margarine
⅔ cup brown sugar
9 slices pineapple
9 maraschino cherries
1¼ cups flour
1 cup sugar
1½ teaspoons baking powder
½ teaspoon salt
¾ cup milk
⅓ cup margarine, softened
1 egg
1 teaspoon vanilla

Preheat oven to 350 degrees F. Melt butter in 8x8-inch baking dish. Sprinkle brown sugar evenly over melted butter. Cut pineapple slices in half and arrange with cherries over sugar-butter mixture. Prepare cake batter by placing remaining ingredients in a mixing bowl and blending on low for 30 seconds. Then beat on high speed, scraping bowl occasionally, for 3 minutes. Pour batter over pineapple topping. Bake for 40 to 45 minutes, until cake tests done. Remove from oven and immediately invert on heat-proof plate. Serve with a dollop of whipped cream. Makes 9 servings.

Variation: In place of pineapple slices, substitute drained crushed pineapple, apricot halves, or sliced peaches.

STING OF THE BEE CAKE

CAKE

1 cup butter (no substitute)
⅔ cup sugar
2 eggs
3 cups sifted flour
3 teaspoons baking powder
1 teaspoon salt
½ cup milk

TOPPING

½ cup butter
1 cup chopped almonds
½ cup sugar
2 tablespoons milk
2 teaspoons vanilla

BUTTER CREAM FILLING

1 cup butter, softened
2 egg yolks
2 cups powdered sugar
2 teaspoons vanilla
½ cup raspberry jam

Prepare Cake: Cream butter; gradually add sugar. Beat in eggs one at a time till light and fluffy. Sift flour, baking powder, and salt; add to creamed mixture alternately with milk. Spoon batter into a well-greased 9-inch springform pan.

Prepare Topping: Melt butter; blend in chopped almonds, sugar, milk, and vanilla. Bring to a boil. Remove from heat and cool slightly. Spread carefully over batter. Bake at 375 degrees F. for 50 minutes or until cake tests done. Remove from oven and cool. Remove sides of springform pan.

Prepare Butter Cream Filling: Whip butter; add egg yolks, powdered sugar, and vanilla.

Assemble Cake: Split cake horizontally into two layers. Put one layer on serving plate. Spread bottom layer with butter cream filling. Spread raspberry jam on top of filling. Replace top layer. Refrigerate. Makes 16 to 20 servings.

GERMAN CHOCOLATE CAKE

1 package milk chocolate cake mix
3 egg yolks
1 cup sugar
1 cup evaporated milk
½ cup butter or margarine
1 teaspoon vanilla
1⅓ cups flaked coconut
1 cup chopped pecans

Preheat oven to 375 degrees F. Grease and flour three 8-inch or two 9-inch round cake pans. Prepare and bake cake according to directions on package. Remove from pans and cool on wire rack. Make frosting by combining egg yolks, sugar, evaporated milk, and butter or margarine in saucepan. Cook and stir over medium heat till thickened, 12 to 15 minutes. Add vanilla, coconut, and pecans. Beat till thick. Spread between layers and on top of cake.

Variation: Frost sides of cake with chocolate frosting, and decorate with maraschino cherries.

BRIGHAM'S BUTTERMILK DOUGHNUTS

2 cups buttermilk
2 large eggs, beaten
1 cup sugar
5 cups sifted flour
2 teaspoons baking soda
1 teaspoon baking powder
1 teaspoon salt
1 teaspoon nutmeg
¼ cup melted butter or shortening
Shortening for frying
½ cup sugar

Combine buttermilk, eggs, and sugar and mix well. Sift flour, baking soda, baking powder, salt, and nutmeg together into a large mixing bowl. Stir in buttermilk mixture, then melted butter. Roll dough out about ¼-inch thick on floured board; cut with doughnut cutter. Fry in hot fat (375 degrees F.) till golden brown on both sides. Drain on paper towels. Place ½ cup sugar in a small paper bag. Place doughnuts, one at a time, in bag and gently toss to cover with sugar. Makes 2 dozen doughnuts.

Note: These doughnuts were reportedly a favorite treat of Brigham Young.

IRRESISTIBLE
COOKIES AND
SWEETS

BRUNE KAGER (Brown Christmas Cookies)

1 cup butter or margarine
1 cup brown sugar
1 cup dark corn syrup
4 cups sifted flour
1 teaspoon cardamom
1 teaspoon cloves
½ teaspoon salt
½ teaspoon allspice
1 teaspoon cinnamon
1 tablespoon grated orange rind
Slivered blanched almonds for tops

Melt butter; add sugar and corn syrup. Remove from heat. Sift flour, cardamom, cloves, salt, allspice, and cinnamon; add to butter-sugar mixture. Stir in orange rind. Mold dough into two long rolls each about 15 inches long. Refrigerate. Dough improves in flavor if allowed to remain in refrigerator for up to three weeks before baking. When ready to bake, cut dough into thin slices and place slices on greased cookie sheet. Decorate each cookie with blanched almonds. Bake at 375 degrees F. for 8 minutes. Cool on wire rack. Store in tightly covered container. Makes 10 dozen cookies.

GINGERBREAD BOY ORNAMENTS

Follow recipe for Brune Kager. After dough is mixed, roll out ½-inch thick on lightly floured surface and cut with gingerbread boy cutter. Place on greased cookie sheet. Press in whole cloves for eyes and raisins for buttons. Poke hole in top with ice pick for ribbon. Bake at 350 degrees F. for 15 minutes. Cool. Thread ribbon through hole and hang cookie in window or on Christmas tree.

JINGLE BELL COOKIE WREATHS

1 cup sugar
1 cup margarine
1 egg
1½ teaspoons almond flavoring
3½ cups flour
1 teaspoon baking powder
¼ teaspoon salt
½ cup milk
Green food coloring
Cinnamon candies

Cream sugar and margarine. Add egg and almond flavoring; beat till fluffy. Sift flour, baking powder, and salt, and add to creamed mixture alternately with milk. Divide dough in half and tint half green, leaving other half white. Chill dough. Sprinkle sugar on work surface. For each wreath, shape 1 teaspoon white dough and 1 teaspoon green dough into 4-inch ropes. Twist ropes together and shape into wreath. Place on ungreased cookie sheet; press 2 or 3 cinnamon candies on each wreath for holly berries. Bake at 375 degrees F. for 9 to 12 minutes. Cool on wire rack. Store in covered container. Makes about 4 dozen wreaths.

GRANDMA'S CHRISTMAS BELL COOKIES

2 cups butter or margarine
1½ cups sugar
2 eggs
1 teaspoon vanilla
5 cups flour
1 teaspoon baking powder
½ teaspoon salt

Cream butter and sugar. Add eggs and vanilla and mix till fluffy. Sift flour, baking powder, and salt, and add to creamed mixture. Refrigerate dough till chilled. Roll out ¼-inch thick on lightly floured board or pastry cloth. Cut with bell-shaped cookie cutter. Place on greased cookie sheet and bake at 350 degrees F. for 12 to 15 minutes. Cool on wire rack. Frost with red- or green-tinted powdered sugar icing. Store in covered container. Makes 5 dozen cookies.

DANISH SHORTBREAD

2 cups butter
1 cup sugar
Pinch of salt
Scant 4 cups sifted flour
1 egg, beaten
Chopped almonds

Whip butter, sugar, and salt till light and fluffy, about 7 to 10 minutes. Add flour gradually, ½ cup at a time, beating after each addition. Roll out about ½-inch thick on floured board or pastry cloth. Cut diagonal in 2-inch lengths; place on ungreased cookie sheet. Press each cookie down slightly with back of fingers. Brush tops with beaten egg. Sprinkle with chopped almonds. Bake at 375 degrees F. for 20 minutes or till light brown. Cool on wire rack. Store in covered container.

GINGER COOKIES

¾ cup shortening
1 cup sugar
¼ cup molasses
1 egg
2 cups flour
2 teaspoons baking soda
¼ teaspoon salt
1½ teaspoons ginger
1 teaspoon cinnamon

Cream shortening and sugar. Add molasses and egg and beat well. Sift flour, baking soda, salt, ginger, and cinnamon, and add gradually to creamed mixture. Chill dough. Mold dough into balls; place on lightly greased cookie sheet. Bake at 350 degrees F. for 8 to 10 minutes. Don't overbake. Cool on wire rack. Store in covered container. Makes 4 dozen cookies.

CHOCOLATE ORANGE LOGS

1 cup butter or margarine
½ cup sifted powdered sugar
1 teaspoon grated orange rind
1 teaspoon orange flavoring
2 cups flour
6 ounces (1 cup) chocolate chips
½ cup finely chopped nuts

Cream butter; gradually add sugar, beating till light and fluffy. Stir in orange rind and orange flavoring. Gradually add flour. Shape dough into a long roll ¾-inch wide; cut roll into 2-inch pieces. Place on greased cookie sheet. Flatten one end of each cookie lengthwise with fork. Bake at 350 degrees F. for 10 minutes, or till light brown. Cool cookies on wire rack. Melt chocolate chips in microwave oven or in top of double boiler over simmering water. Dip unflattened ends of cookies in chocolate; then roll in chopped nuts. Store in covered container. Makes 4 dozen cookies.

NORTH POLE NUGGETS

½ cup butter
½ cup shortening
½ cup sugar
1 teaspoon almond extract
2 cups sifted flour
Red and green maraschino cherries

Cream butter, shortening, and sugar. Add almond extract and flour; blend well. Shape dough into balls, using 1 tablespoon of dough for each cookie. Place on greased cookie sheet. Make indentation in center of each cookie and press maraschino cherry into top. Bake at 350 degrees F. for 8 to 10 minutes. Cool on wire rack. Store in covered container. Makes 2½ dozen.

KRIS KRINKLES

½ cup shortening
1⅔ cups sugar
2 eggs
2 teaspoons vanilla
2 squares unsweetened chocolate,
  melted
2¼ cups sifted flour
1 teaspoon salt
⅓ cup milk
½ cup chopped walnuts
Sifted powdered sugar

Cream shortening and sugar together till light and fluffy. Add eggs and vanilla and beat well. Add melted chocolate. Add flour and salt alternately with milk. Stir in nuts. Chill thoroughly 3 to 4 hours or overnight. Form into 1-inch balls and roll each ball lightly in powdered sugar. Place on greased cookie sheet about 2 to 3 inches apart. Bake at 350 degrees F. for 12 to 15 minutes. Cool slightly before removing from pan. Continue cooling on wire rack. Makes 45 cookies.

DATE PINWHEELS

2 cups chopped dates
1 cup sugar
1 cup water
1 cup chopped nuts
1 cup margarine
2 cups brown sugar
3 eggs
4 cups flour
½ teaspoon salt
½ teaspoon baking soda

Mix dates, sugar, and water together in small saucepan and cook 10 minutes. Mix in nuts and cool. In a large mixing bowl, cream margarine and brown sugar. Beat in eggs. Sift together flour, salt, and bakingsoda; stir into creamed mixture (dough will be stiff). Divide dough in half; chill 1 hour or till dough can be rolled easily. On lightly floured surface, roll dough out into two 10x15-inch rectangles.

Spread each rectngle with half of date filling. Carefully roll up jelly-roll style, beginning at long side. Wrap each roll in wax paper and refrigerate several hours. Cut into ¼-inch slices. Place on greased cookie sheet. Bake at 375 degrees F. about 12 minutes. Remove from cookie sheet and cool on wire rack. Store in covered container. Makes 6 dozen cookies.

JOLLY JUMBO OATMEAL COOKIES

1 cup shortening or margarine
1 cup brown sugar
1 cup sugar
2 eggs
1 teaspoon vanilla
2 cups flour
½ teaspoon baking soda
½ teaspoon salt
1 teaspoon cinnamon
½ teaspoon cloves
½ teaspoon ginger
3 cups quick-cooking oats
1 cup walnuts, chopped

Cream shortening and sugars till fluffy. Add eggs and continue beating. Add vanilla. Sift flour, baking soda, salt, cinnamon, cloves, and ginger together and add gradually to creamed mixture. Stir in oatmeal and nuts. Measure ¼ cup dough for each cookie and place on greased cookie sheet, about 4 inches apart. Bake at 350 degrees F. for 12 to 15 minutes, until light brown. Carefully remove from cookie sheet. Cool. Store in covered container. Makes 28 cookies.

Variations: Add raisins, chocolate chips, cut-up gumdrops, or M&M candies to dough and bake as directed.

THORA'S BUTTERSCOTCH COOKIES

½ cup butter or margarine
1½ cups brown sugar
2 eggs
1 teaspoon vanilla
2⅔ cups flour
1 teaspoon baking soda
½ teaspoon baking powder
½ teaspoon salt
1 cup sour cream
1 cup chopped pecans

FROSTING
½ cup butter
3 cups powdered sugar
¼ cup hot water
Pecan halves

Cream butter and brown sugar; add eggs and vanilla and beat well. Sift flour, baking soda, baking powder, and salt, and add to creamed mixture alternately with sour cream. Fold in chopped nuts. Drop by spoonful onto greased cookie sheet. Bake at 350 degrees F. for 10 minutes. Cool on wire rack. After frosting cookies, store them in covered container.

Make frosting: Cook butter in saucepan over medium heat till bubbly and golden brown. Beat in powdered sugar and hot water. Frost cooled cookies and top each with a pecan half. Makes 5 dozen cookies.

MILLION–DOLLAR COOKIES

2 cups shortening
1 cup white sugar
1 cup brown sugar
2 eggs
1 teaspoon vanilla
1 teaspoon almond flavoring
4 cups flour
2 teaspoons baking soda
2 teaspoons cream of tartar

Cream shortening, sugars, eggs, vanilla, and almond flavoring till fluffy. Sift flour, baking soda, and cream of tartar together and add gradually to creamed mixture. Chill dough. Mold dough into 1-inch balls. Place onto greased cookie sheet. Flatten each cookie with bottom of drinking glass dipped in sugar. Bake 10 minutes at 350 degrees F. Cool on wire rack. Store in covered container. Makes 5 dozen cookies.

Variations: Add chocolate chips, chopped nuts, or raisins to batter before chilling. Drop by spoonfuls onto cookie sheet, and bake as above.

HONEY CHOCOLATE DROPS

1 cup shortening
⅔ cup honey
2 eggs, slightly beaten
1 teaspoon baking soda
¼ cup water
2 teaspoons vanilla
2⅔ cups flour
1 teaspoon salt
1 cup chocolate chips
½ cup chopped walnuts

Cream shortening and honey till blended. Add eggs and beat till fluffy. Dissolve baking soda in ¼ cup water and add to mixture. Add vanilla. Sift flour and salt and add to mixture. Mix in chocolate chips and nuts. Drop by spoonfuls onto ungreased cookie sheet. Bake at 375 degrees F. for 10 minutes. Cool on wire rack. Store in covered container. Makes 4 dozen cookies.

OATMEAL FUDGE BARS

1 cup margarine
2 cups brown sugar
2 eggs
2 teaspoons vanilla
2½ cups flour
1 teaspoon baking soda
½ teaspoon salt
1½ cups quick-cooking oats
1 14-ounce can sweetened condensed
  milk
1 12-ounce package semisweet
  chocolate chips
¼ cup margarine
2 teaspoons vanilla
1 cup chopped walnuts (optional)

Cream margarine and brown sugar; add eggs and vanilla. Sift flour, baking soda, and salt; add to creamed mixture. Mix in oatmeal. In heavy saucepan mix sweetened condensed milk, chocolate chips, and margarine and heat till just melted. Stir in vanilla and nuts. Spread ⅔ of the cookie dough into 9x13-inch greased baking pan. Spread with chocolate mixture. Drop remaining ⅓ dough on top. Bake at 350 degrees F. for 25 minutes. Cool; then cut into bars. Makes 36 bars.

BUTTER PECAN SQUARES

½ cup butter, softened
½ cup packed brown sugar
1 egg
1 teaspoon vanilla
¾cup flour
2 cups milk chocolate chips
¾ cup chopped pecans

Cream butter, sugar, egg, and vanilla till light and fluffy. Blend in flour. Stir in 1 cup chocolate chips and ½ cup pecans. Pour into greased 8-inch square baking dish. Bake at 350 degrees F. for 25 to 30 minutes. Remove from oven and immediately sprinkle with remaining 1 cup chips. When chips melt, spread evenly over top with knife. Sprinkle with ¼ cup pecans; cool, then cut into squares. Makes 16 bars.

JOLLY ELF GRANOLA BARS

1 14-ounce package chocolate
  caramels
2 tablespoons water
¾ cup crunchy peanut butter
3 cups plain granola
1 cup golden raisins
½ cup salted peanuts

Melt caramels and water over medium heat in heavy saucepan, stirring often (or melt in glass dish in microwave oven). Stir in peanut butter. Add granola, raisins, and peanuts; mix well. Pour into a buttered 9x13-inch pan, and cool. Cut into 1x2-inch bars. Makes about 32 bars.

Variation: Substitute plain caramels for chocolate caramels.

CATHY'S BROWNIES

1 cup butter or margarine
½ cup cocoa
4 eggs
2 cups sugar
1 teaspoon vanilla
1½ cups flour
½ teaspoon salt
½ teaspoon baking soda
¾ cup chopped nuts

FROSTING

¼ cup cocoa
¼ cup butter or margarine
5 tablespoons milk
3 cups powdered sugar

Melt 1 cup butter and stir in ½ cup cocoa. Cool. Beat eggs; gradually add sugar a little at a time. Add vanilla and chocolate mixture. Sift together the flour, salt, and baking soda; add to creamed mixture. Stir in nuts. Pour into 9x13-inch greased baking pan. Bake at 350 degrees F. for about 30 minutes, till wooden pick inserted comes out clean. Cool.

Make frosting by melting butter and stirring in cocoa. Add milk and beat in powdered sugar to spreading consistency. Pour and spread over cooled brownies. Frosting will become more firm as it cools. Cut into bars. Makes 2 dozen brownies.

Brownie Sundaes: For each serving, place an unfrosted brownie on a dessert plate. Top with a scoop of vanilla ice cream, drizzle with chocolate sauce, and add a dollop of whipped cream and a green or red cherry. Garnish with a sprig of holly.

LAYERED CREAM-CHEESE BROWNIES

1 8-ounce package cream cheese,
   softened
1/3 cup sugar
1 egg
1 or 2 tablespoons milk
1 cup water
1 cup margarine
5 tablespoons cocoa
2 squares baking chocolate
4 eggs
2 cups sugar
1/2 cup buttermilk
1 teaspoon baking soda
1 teaspoon vanilla
3 cups flour

Whip cream cheese, sugar, egg, and milk till fluffy; set aside. In small saucepan, heat water, margarine, cocoa, and chocolate till melted. In large mixing bowl, beat eggs and sugar. Mix in chocolate-water mixture, then add buttermilk, baking soda, vanilla, and flour; mix well. Pour half of batter into a 12x17-inch greased cookie sheet. Spoon cream cheese mixture evenly over top of batter. Pour remaining chocolate batter over cream cheese. Bake at 350 degrees F. for 30 minutes. Remove from oven and cool. Spread with Cream Cheese Icing. Makes 42 2x2½-inch brownies.

CREAM CHEESE ICING

1 3-ounce package cream
   cheese, softened
1/4 cup margarine
3 cups powdered sugar
3 tablespoons cocoa
1 teaspoon vanilla
1 to 2 tablespoons milk

Make icing by whipping cream cheese and margarine; add powdered sugar, cocoa, and vanilla with a little milk till spreading consistency. Spread over cooled brownies.

PEANUT BUTTER FINGERS

½ cup butter or margarine
½ cup white sugar
½ cup brown sugar
1 egg
⅓ cup peanut butter
½ teaspoon baking soda
¼ teaspoon salt
½ teaspoon vanilla
1 cup flour
1 cup quick-cooking oats

TOPPING
1 6-ounce package chocolate chips
½ cup sifted powdered sugar
¼ cup peanut butter
1 to 2 tablespoons milk

Cream butter and white and brown sugars. Blend in egg, ⅓ cup peanut butter, baking soda, salt, and vanilla. Stir in flour and oatmeal. Pour into a greased 9x13-inch baking pan and bake at 350 degrees F. for 20 to 25 minutes.

While bars are cooking, *prepare topping:* Cream powdered sugar, ¼ cup peanut butter, and enough milk to make mixture spreading consistency.

Remove pan from oven and sprinkle bars with chocolate chips. Let stand 5 minutes, then spread like frosting. With knife or spatula, swirl peanut butter frosting over chocolate topping. Cool thoroughly, then cut into 24 bars.

COCONUT CHEWS

½ cup butter
1 cup flour
2 tablespoons sugar
Pinch of salt
1½ cups brown sugar
2 eggs
2 teaspoons vanilla
1 cup flaked coconut
1 cup chopped nuts

Cut butter into flour, sugar, and salt with pastry blender. Press into 8x12-inch baking pan. Bake at 350 degrees F. for 15 minutes. While crust is baking, prepare topping: Beat brown sugar and eggs together till smooth. Add vanilla, coconut, and nuts. Carefully spread over baked crust, then return to oven and continue baking for 25 minutes longer. Cut into squares while warm. Cool, then cover pan to store. Makes 24 bars.

LION HOUSE PECAN BARS

¾ cup butter or margarine
¾ cup sugar
2 eggs
3 cups flour
½ teaspoon baking powder
Grated rind of 1 lemon
1 cup butter or margarine
1 cup brown sugar
1 cup honey
¼ cup light cream
3 cups pecans, chopped

Cream ¾ cup butter and sugar; add eggs and beat well. Blend in flour, baking powder, and lemon rind. Press dough into a greased 9x13-inch pan. Prick with fork. Bake 12 to 15 minutes at 375 degrees F. Make topping by mixing 1 cup butter, brown sugar, and honey in saucepan. Stir and boil 5 minutes. Cool slightly and add cream and chopped pecans. Spread over partially baked crust. Return to oven and bake 30 to 35 minutes, reducing oven temperature to 350 degrees F. Cool and cut into bars. Makes 42 small bars.

MOLDED ANIMAL LOLLIPOPS

2 cups sugar
⅔ cup water
⅔ cup corn syrup
½ teaspoon oil flavoring, such as
  cinnamon, peppermint, or fruit
Food coloring

Grease lollipop molds with spray vegetable shortening, and arrange them on a cookie sheet that has also been sprayed. Cook sugar, water, and corn syrup in heavy saucepan over high heat, stirring till sugar dissolves. Reduce heat and continue cooking to hard-crack stage. Remove from heat and stir in flavoring and coloring. Spoon syrup into lollipop molds with wooden sticks inserted. When lollipops cool, wrap in plastic wrap. Makes approximately 25 lollipops.

Variation: Place wooden sticks on greased cookie sheet and pour about 1 tablespoon syrup on end of each stick to make round lollipops. While candy is still hot and sticky, decorate with gumdrops cut in pieces, cinnamon candies, commercial cake decorations, or frosting.

LUSCIOUS FUDGE

1 12-ounce milk chocolate bar, broken
   in pieces
2 cups semisweet chocolate chips
1 7-ounce jar marshmallow creme
1 12-ounce can evaporated milk
4½ cups sugar
⅛ teaspoon salt
2 teaspoons vanilla
2 cups chopped walnuts

Combine milk chocolate bar pieces, chocolate chips, and marshmallow creme in large mixing bowl. In heavy saucepan, mix evaporated milk, sugar, and salt. Bring to boil over medium heat and boil for six minutes. Pour over chocolate mixture. Beat vigorously with wooden spoon till creamy. Add vanilla and chopped walnuts. Mix well. Pour into buttered 9x13-inch pan. Let stand two hours, then cut into squares. Makes 5 pounds candy.

OLD-FASHIONED FUDGE

3 cups sugar
3 tablespoons cocoa
3 tablespoons corn syrup
1 cup light cream
2 tablespoons butter
1 teaspoon vanilla
½ cup nuts

Cook sugar, cocoa, corn syrup, and cream in heavy saucepan till just a little past soft-ball stage. Remove from heat and add butter and vanilla. Cool; then beat till candy loses its gloss and thickens. Add nuts and pour into 8-inch square greased pan. Cool, then cut into squares. Makes 64 pieces of candy.

CHRISTMAS CARAMELS

1 cup butter
1 cup brown sugar
1 cup white sugar
1 cup light corn syrup
1 14-ounce can sweetened condensed
   milk
Dash of salt

Combine ingredients in heavy pan. Cook over medium heat, stirring constantly with wooden spoon. Keep at rolling boil and cook till soft ball forms in cold water (about 15 minutes). Pour into buttered 7x11-inch pan. Cool, then cut into squares and wrap each piece in wax paper. Makes about 75 pieces of candy.

CARAMEL TURTLES

2 cups sugar
2 cups light corn syrup
2 cups light cream
½ teaspoon salt
¾ cup evaporated milk
6 tablespoons butter
Pecan halves

In heavy saucepan mix sugar, corn syrup, cream, and salt. Bring to boil and cook to soft-ball stage. Slowly, so boiling doesn't stop, add evaporated milk and butter. Continue cooking till about 238 degrees F. (247 degrees F. at sea level). Arrange pecans in clusters on wax paper on baking sheet. Drop spoonful of caramel onto each pecan cluster. Cool. Dip candies in chocolate, if desired. Makes 2½ pounds of candy.

PULLED PEANUT BRITTLE

2 cups sugar
1 cup corn syrup
1 cup water
1 cup peanuts
1 cup flaked coconut
¼ cup butter
1 teaspoon vanilla
1½ teaspoons baking soda

Mix sugar, corn syrup, and water together in heavy saucepan, stirring till dissolved. Bring to boil. Cook to 275 degrees F. (284 degrees F. at sea level) on candy thermometer. Add peanuts and coconut and continue cooking to 300 degrees F. (309 degrees F. at sea level). Remove from heat and add butter and vanilla. Add baking soda and stir quickly (candy will foam up). Quickly pour out onto a large buttered baking sheet. Stretch and pull candy out with fingers (wear rubber gloves to avoid burns) till thin. When cool, break into pieces.

NOEL NOUGATS

¼ cup water
2 cups sugar
2¼ cups white corn syrup
Whites of 3 small eggs
½ teaspoon vanilla
¼ teaspoon salt
4 tablespoons butter
2 teaspoons flour

Mix water, sugar, and corn syrup in heavy saucepan. Cook to 232 degrees F. (241 degrees F. at sea level). In the meantime, beat egg whites till stiff. Pour ⅓ of the syrup over egg whites and continue beating on low speed of electric mixer. Cook remaining syrup to 258 degrees F. (267 degrees F. at sea level); add slowly to egg-white mixture and continue beating till stiff, about 5 minutes. Add vanilla. Fold in melted butter and flour. Do not stir much after butter has been added. Pour out onto oiled marble slab or cookie sheet. Cool. Cut into pieces or use as centers for pecan rolls. Can also be used as centers when dipping chocolates.

Variation: Just before pouring candy out, add chopped nuts and cut-up maraschino cherries. Makes 2 pounds candy.

BUTTER FONDANT

6 cups sugar
2¼ cups cream
¼ cup butter
2 tablespoons white corn syrup
Dash of salt

1. In heavy saucepan, dissolve sugar with cream and bring to boil. Add butter, corn syrup, and salt. Cover and cook for three minutes to wash down sides of pan. Remove cover and continue cooking without stirring to soft ball stage, or 230 degrees F. (239 degrees F. at sea level). Without scraping saucepan, immediately pour fondant onto buttered, cold marble slab, baking sheet, or Formica.

2. When cool to touch, beat candy with paddle. When fondant loses gloss, let rest for 20 minutes; then knead, like bread, till fondant is soft and all lumps are out. Store in covered container till ready to dip. (Can be stored for up to a month.) Makes 3 pounds of fondant.

3. When ready to dip, divide fondant into small amounts. Knead in different flavors and colors, such as rum, black walnut, orange, lemon, cherry, or mint. Chopped nuts can be added at this time. Chill, then shape into centers for dipping.

4. To dip chocolates, melt dipping chocolate in top of double boiler on low heat. With fork, dip fondant centers into chocolate, then place on wax paper. When cool, store in covered containers. When dipping chocolates, room temperature should be cool, about 60 degrees F.

Variation: Different colored coatings are also available for dipping.

LICORICE CARAMELS

1 14-ounce can sweetened condensed
    milk
1 cup sugar
1 cup butter (or ½ cup butter and ½
    cup margarine)
½ teaspoon salt
1½ cups white corn syrup
Anise flavoring or licorice oil
Black food coloring

Combine sweetened condensed milk, sugar, butter, salt, and corn syrup in heavy saucepan and bring to boil. Add ½ bottle licorice oil or 2 capfuls anise flavoring and ½ ounce black food coloring. Continue cooking till firm-ball stage, or 234 degrees F. (243 degrees F. at sea level). Remove from heat and pour into 8-inch-square buttered pan. Refrigerate till cool. Cut and wrap each piece in wax paper or plastic wrap.

Note: If candy goes too hard, add 1 additional can of sweetened condensed milk and cook again.

Variation: For strawberry caramels, follow same recipe but use 3 capfuls of strawberry flavoring in place of anise. Use red food coloring in place of black.

BAVARIAN MINTS

1 pound milk chocolate
1 square (1 ounce) unsweetened
 chocolate
1 14-ounce can sweetened condensed
 milk
2 tablespoons butter
Few drops vanilla
3 to 8 drops oil of peppermint

In top of double boiler melt milk chocolate, unsweetened chocolate, sweetened condensed milk, and butter. Stir till smooth; remove from heat. Add vanilla and oil of peppermint to taste. Pour into buttered 8-inch-square pan. Cool. Cut into one-inch squares. Makes 64 pieces of candy.

CHOCOLATE ALMOND BALLS

1 8-ounce chocolate bar with almonds
1 8-ounce container frozen whipped
 topping, thawed
30 vanilla wafers, crushed

Melt chocolate bar over warm water. Cool slightly (but not cold). Stir in whipped topping, which is at room temperature. Roll in balls about 1 teaspoon in size, and roll in vanilla wafer crumbs. Keep in freezer for two hours before serving. Store in freezer. Makes about 4 dozen.

CHOCOLATE TRUFFLES

½ cup whipping cream
⅓ cup sugar
6 tablespoons butter
1 cup semisweet chocolate chips
1 teaspoon vanilla

COATING

2 cups semisweet chocolate chips
2 tablespoons shortening

1. Mix cream, sugar, and butter in saucepan and bring to boil. Remove from heat. Add 1 cup chocolate chips and stir till chips are melted. Add vanilla. Pour into bowl and cool, stirring occasionally. Cover and chill in refrigerator several hours or overnight to allow mixture to ripen and harden.

2. Remove from refrigerator and form into ½-inch balls, working quickly to prevent melting. Place on wax paper on cookie sheet. Chill again several hours.

3. To make chocolate coating, melt 2 cups chocolate chips with shortening in top of double boiler. Remove from heat and cool to 85 degrees F., stirring constantly. Dip each truffle into chocolate with fork; gently tap fork on side of bowl to remove excess coating. Invert candies onto wax paper. Makes about 30 truffles.

POPCORN–NUT CRUNCH

3 quarts popped corn
1⅓ cups pecan halves
⅔ cup almonds
½ cup white corn syrup
1⅓ cups sugar
1 cup butter
½ teaspoon cream of tartar
1 tablespoon vanilla
1 teaspoon baking soda
4 cups miniature mashmallows, frozen

Mix popcorn, pecans, and almonds in large bowl or pan. In saucepan, combine corn syrup, sugar, butter, and cream of tartar. Cook and stir till mixture comes to a boil. Reduce heat to medium and boil 10 minutes (hardball stage). Stir in vanilla and baking soda. Pour over popcorn and nuts, stirring to coat evenly. Add frozen marshmallows and continue stirring till mixture is evenly coated with syrup. Spread on buttered cookie sheets to cool. Break into chunks and store in airtight container.

QUICK CARAMEL CORN

2 gallons popped corn (1 cup
  unpopped)
½ cup butter
2 cups brown sugar
½ cup light corn syrup
1 tablespoon water
Pinch of baking soda

Place popped corn in large pan. Melt butter in saucepan. Add brown sugar, corn syrup, and water. Cook and stir till mixture reaches hard boil. Add a pinch of baking soda. Remove from heat and pour over popcorn. Stir to coat thoroughly. Cool; then break into clusters. Store in covered container.

Hint: Place popcorn in heavy brown grocery bag; pour over syrup; close bag and knead the bag with both hands till corn is well-coated.

HONEY TAFFY POPCORN

1 cup sugar
½ cup light honey
½ cup cream
⅛ teaspoon baking soda
1 teaspoon vanilla
4 quarts popped corn

Mix sugar, honey, and cream in heavy saucepan. Cook over medium heat to 260 degrees F. (269 degrees F. at sea level). Remove from heat and stir in baking soda, stirring till bubbles subside; add vanilla. Pour over popped corn that has been lightly salted and buttered. Stir till coated. Cool and break into chunks.

ENGLISH TOFFEE

1 cup butter
5 teaspoons water
1 cup sugar
1 teaspoon vanilla
*½ cup Toasted Almonds (recipe
  below)*
1 8-ounce milk chocolate bar
*½ cup finely chopped walnuts
  (optional)*

In a heavy saucepan mix butter, water, and sugar. Bring to boil and cook at highest heat, stirring constantly, until golden brown and candy leaves sides of pan. Remove from heat and add vanilla and toasted almonds. Pour onto greased cookie sheet. Break up chocolate bar into small pieces and sprinkle over top of toffee. When chocolate starts to melt, spread evenly over top of toffee with knife. Sprinkle with walnuts, if desired. Allow to cool for 12 hours. Break into pieces. Makes about 1½ pounds candy.

TOASTED ALMONDS

Spread 1 cup blanched slivered almonds in shallow pan and coat with 1 teaspoon salad oil or melted butter. Roast in oven at 300 degrees F. for 15 to 20 minutes, stirring often.

MOLASSES TAFFY

1 cup molasses (or honey, if desired)
1 cup whipping cream
1 cup sugar

In heavy saucepan, mix molasses, cream, and sugar. Bring to boil. Cook to 260 degrees F. at sea level, or hard-ball stage. Remove from heat and pour onto buttered cookie sheet. Cool till lukewarm and can be handled comfortably. Take a small piece of taffy at a time and stretch and fold, stretch and fold, till taffy turns light and pliable. Form into twisted ropes and cut into pieces with scissors. Wrap each piece of candy in wax paper or plastic wrap. Makes 1½ pounds of candy.

VINEGAR TAFFY

2 cups sugar
2 tablespoons corn syrup
2 tablespoons butter
½ cup vinegar
⅛ teaspoon cream of tartar
Pinch of salt

In heavy saucepan combine all six ingredients. Stir till sugar is dissolved. Cook to about 260 degrees F. at sea level, or hard-ball stage. Remove from heat and pour onto buttered cookie sheet. Cool till lukewarm and can be handled comfortably. Take a small piece of taffy at a time and stretch and fold till taffy turns light and pliable. Form into twisted ropes and cut into pieces with scissors. Wrap in wax paper or plastic wrap. Makes 72 pieces.

SUGAR-GLAZED PEANUTS

2 cups raw Spanish peanuts
1 cup sugar
½ cup water
Salt

Combine peanuts, sugar, and water in heavy saucepan. Cook over medium heat till mixture crystallizes and coats peanuts, about 10 to 15 minutes. Remove from heat and spread mixture out onto 2 large greased cookie sheets. Sprinkle with salt. Bake for 15 minutes at 300 degrees F. Stir and bake for 15 more minutes. Cool and break apart. Makes 4 cups of peanuts.

PATIENCE

3 cups sugar
3 cups evaporated milk
½ cup chopped walnuts

Put 1 cup of the sugar in heavy skillet and place on low heat. Stir continually till sugar caramelizes and turns light brown. Add 1 cup of the evaporated milk. Sugar will harden into a lump; stir and cook till smooth and free from lumps. Then slowly add 1 more cup sugar; then 1 cup milk; 1 cup sugar; and finally the last cup of milk. Stir continuously till firm-ball stage is reached. Add nuts and drop by teaspoon onto buttered cookie sheet. Makes about 2 pounds of candy.

Note: Candy is called Patience because of the patience required to cook and stir after each addition.

AUNT BILL'S BROWN CANDY

3 cups sugar
1 cup light cream
¼ teaspoon baking soda
¼ cup butter
⅛ teaspoon salt
1 teaspoon vanilla
½ cup chopped pecans

Put 1 cup of the sugar in heavy skillet and place on low heat. Stir continually till sugar caramelizes and turns light brown. In the meantime mix the remaining 2 cups of sugar and cream in heavy saucepan and place on low heat. Slowly pour the caramelized sugar in a fine stream into the sugar and cream mixture, stirring continuously. Cook and stir over low heat till mixture forms a firm ball when tested in cold water. Remove from heat and immediately add baking soda, stirring vigorously. Add butter and salt and let stand 20 minutes. Add vanilla and begin beating. Using a wooden spoon, beat till mixture is thick and heavy and has a dull appearance instead of a glossy sheen. Add chopped nuts and turn into a buttered pan. When slightly cool, cut into squares. Candy stays moist indefinitely if stored in covered container in refrigerator. Makes 2 pounds candy.

Gifts from the Kitchen
Assorted jams, jellies, candies, breads, muffins, and other delicious gifts to
delight loved ones and friends during the holiday season (see pages 189-208)

HOLIDAY DIVINITY

3 cups sugar
1 cup corn syrup
½ cup water
2 egg whites (room temperature)
1 teaspoon vanilla
Red food coloring
⅓ cup chopped maraschino cherries
½ cup chopped pecans

Mix sugar, corn syrup, and water in a saucepan and bring to boil. Cover pan for 3 minutes or until steam inside the pan has melted sugar crystals down from sides. Remove cover and continue cooking without stirring until syrup spins a long thread when tested with a spoon (about 254 degrees F. at sea level). While syrup is cooking, place egg whites in a large bowl and beat until they are just stiff enough to hold their shape. When syrup is done, pour over the egg whites in a fine stream, beating vigorously. Do not scrape pan. Add vanilla and 2 or 3 drops of red food coloring to tint pink. Continue beating until candy is thick and creamy and holds its shape. Stir in cherries and pecans. Drop from a teaspoon onto waxed paper. Divinity does not keep well, so plan to serve it while it is fresh. Makes 4 dozen pieces.

BUTTER CREAM MINTS

1 cup water
½ cup butter
2 cups sugar
Oil of peppermint or
  1 teaspoon mint extract
Food coloring

In heavy 3-quart saucepan heat water and butter until butter is melted. Add sugar and stir with wooden spoon until dissolved. Cover and bring to boil. Remove lid and wipe sides of pan with brush to remove any sugar crystals. Continue cooking until syrup reaches 260 degrees F. (sea level). Pour onto cold buttered slab. Do not scrape pan. Sprinkle with 6 drops of oil of peppermint and 2 or 3 drops of desired food coloring, but do not stir in. When cool enough to handle, pull like taffy until candy is firm but elastic and loses its gloss. Pull out to a ½-inch rope; cut into ½-inch pieces. Store in covered container. Candy will mellow in 12 to 24 hours. Makes 90 mints.

GIFTS FROM
THE KITCHEN

GIFTS OF FOOD

Sharing is the heart of Christmas: sharing love, sharing gifts, sharing traditions, and sharing food. Gifts of food, prepared in your own kitchen, convey warmth, individuality, and good eating. In this section are recipes perfect for sharing the cheer of the season with the special people in your life.

Make your gift of food serve a dual purpose by packaging it in a practical kitchen utensil. Tempting holiday delicacies from your kitchen, combined with useful household items, serve as lasting reminders of your thoughtfulness. Colorful wrappings and trim — using cellophane or plastic wrap — will keep the foods fresh and eye-appealing till served.

1. Fill glass cruets with homemade salad dressings.

2. In a gleaming copper mold, present a Bundt cake or homemade nut torte.

3. Choose a simple glass compote and heap it with Coco-Date Balls, Chocolate Orange Logs, or Butter Pecan Squares.

4. Give a practical pie plate in a wicker holder and filled with your fussiest holiday pie, like Chocolate Angel Pie.

5. Fill a fancy jam pot with Cranberry Conserves and seal with paraffin.

6. Give a handsome soufflé or casserole dish filled with your finest Christmas cookies and gaily bedecked with tiny ornaments and ribbon.

7. Fill a fancy basket with muffins, such as Gold Rush Muffins — a mouth-watering and nutritious snack-time treat.

8. Create an eye-catching basket of fruit and cheese for Christmas giving. As a thoughtful touch, include a handy cheese cutter.

9. Hearty Granary Bread straight from the oven is a marvelous gift on a sturdy cutting board, both useful and decorative.

10. Colorful crockery mugs are handy for gifts of dips, dunks, or breadsticks.

BOUQUET GARNI

½ cup dehydrated parsley flakes
¼ cup dried thyme leaves
¼ cup dehydrated celery flakes
2 tablespoons marjoram leaves
5 bay leaves, crushed

Mix herbs together in small bowl. Cut 16 4-inch squares of cheesecloth. Place 1 tablespoon herb mixture in center of each square. Bring corners together and tie bundle with string. Store in an airtight container in a cool, dark place. Use to flavor stock for soups and sauces, and for poaching fish and chicken. Drop one packet into 1 quart of stock; simmer at least 20 minutes or according to recipe directions. Remove packet and discard before serving.

Gift Container: Arrange packets in a small flowerpot, basket, or recipe card box. Write the directions for use and storage on a recipe card to include with the gift.

OYSTER CRACKER SNACKS

1 1-pound box oyster crackers
1 package dry ranch-style dressing mix
1 teaspoon dill weed
½ teaspoon lemon pepper
½ cup vegetable or butter-flavored oil

Pour crackers into large bowl. Combine dressing mix with dill weed and lemon pepper, and sprinkle over crackers. Pour oil over crackers, stirring till oil is absorbed. Spread on cookie sheet and bake at 250 degrees F. for 15 minutes; cool.

Gift Container: Fill soup mugs with Oyster Cracker Snacks. Cover with plastic wrap and tie with gift ribbon.

CANDIED CITRUS PEEL

3 oranges
1 grapefruit
6 cups water
1½ cups sugar
1 tablespoon light corn syrup
½ teaspoon ground ginger
1 envelope unflavored gelatin
⅓ cup water

Microwave Directions: Quarter oranges and grapefruit and remove peel in sections. (Save fruit for another use.) Trim most of the white membrane from peel. Cut peel into ¼-inch-wide strips. Combine peel and 2 cups of the water in glass casserole dish. Cover. Microcook on HIGH 10 minutes. Drain. Repeat 2 more times, adding 2 cups fresh water and microcooking each time, as above. Drain. Stir in 1 cup of the sugar, corn syrup, ginger, gelatin, and ⅓ cup water. Microcook on HIGH, uncovered, 11 to 12 minutes or till about half the liquid is absorbed, stirring every 4 minutes. Cool slightly. Sprinkle remaining ½ cup sugar on wax paper.

Remove peel from syrup a few strips at a time and roll in the sugar. Place on wax paper and allow to dry overnight. Store in tightly covered container. Makes ½ pound.

Gift Container: Layer peel in an apothecary or candy jar and seal with tape.

Conventional Cooking Directions: Simmer peel and water in saucepan 10 minutes. Drain. Repeat 2 more times. Drain. Mix 1 cup sugar, corn syrup, ginger, gelatin, and ⅓ cup water. Add peel and simmer, uncovered, for 15 minutes, stirring occasionally. Cook slightly and roll in sugar as above.

ORANGE-SPICE NUTS

2 tablespoons butter or margarine
¼ cup packed brown sugar
½ teaspoon cinnamon
¼ teaspoon salt
¼ teaspoon nutmeg
¼ teaspoon grated orange peel
1 tablespoon water
2 cups walnuts, pecans, or blanched almonds

Microwave Directions: In a glass bowl, microcook butter till melted, about 30 seconds. Add remaining ingredients and stir till nuts are coated. Microcook on HIGH, uncovered, 4 to 5 minutes or till nuts are toasted and glazed, stirring 2 to 3 times. Spoon nuts onto wax paper. Separate with fork. Cool. Makes 2½ cups.

Gift Container: Place nuts in an airtight container lined with cellophane or a paper doily. Or place them in a plastic bag and enclose the bag in a fabric drawstring bag or Christmas stocking.

Conventional Cooking: In heavy pan over medium heat, melt butter. Add remaining ingredients and stir till nuts are coated. Cook, uncovered, till nuts are toasted and glazed, stirring occasionally. Spoon nuts onto wax paper, and separate with fork. Cool.

HERBED VINEGAR

Fresh Herbs: Place sprigs of fresh herbs, such as basil, tarragon, dill, or rosemary, in a small bottle or cruet; fill with white, cider, or wine vinegar. Cover with lid, cap, or cork. Let stand at room temperature at least 5 days to blend flavors.

Dried Herbs: Mix ½ cup dried herbs (such as rosemary, thyme, tarragon, oregano, basil, or dill), 1 clove crushed garlic, and 1 quart vinegar. Pour into bottles or cruets. Cap tightly and let stand as directed above.

Garlic-Parsley: Place 2 cloves garlic, peeled and speared on wooden skewer, and 3 sprigs fresh parsley in bottle. Fill with vinegar. Cap and let stand as directed above.

Directions for Use: Sprinkle herbed vinegars directly on salads. Or make a basic vinaigrette using 1 part herbed vinegar to 3 parts oil plus salt and pepper to taste.

Gift Container: Combine the gift bottle or cruet of herbed vinegar with a cruet of olive oil, and put them in a wire salad basket or a wooden salad bowl.

SWEET 'N' HOT MUSTARD

1 cup sugar
⅔ cup dry mustard
3 eggs, well beaten
⅔ cup white vinegar

In a medium saucepan, whisk together sugar and mustard till well blended. Add eggs and vinegar, blending well. Cook over low heat, stirring till thickened. Cool. Spoon into gift containers. Cover and refrigerate up to 1 month. Serve with ham, corned beef, cold cuts, or cheese.

Gift Container: Select baby food jars, pimiento jars, or small crocks. Be sure lids are tightly closed or secured with tape. Decorate each jar with ribbon and attach a wooden mustard spoon. Pack in a basket with an assortment of cold cuts, cheese, and crackers. Attach directions for storage.

ROQUEFORT CHEESE LOG

1 8-ounce package cream cheese
1 5-ounce jar sharp cheese spread
1 cup grated sharp Cheddar cheese
½ cup (4 ounces) Roquefort cheese,
  crumbled
¼ cup light cream
1 teaspoon grated onion
Few drops hot pepper sauce
1 cup chopped walnuts

Bring cheeses to room temperature. In small mixing bowl, combine cheeses with cream, onion, and hot pepper sauce. Blend well. Taste for seasoning and correct, if needed. Cover and chill for 3 hours or overnight. Shape into log or ball, using wet hands for final shaping. Roll in nuts. Cover with plastic wrap and refrigerate up to 2 weeks. Remove from refrigerator about 30 minutes before serving.

Gift Container: Securely wrap the log in plastic wrap and place in a basket or tie onto a cutting board with ribbon. Include on a gift tag or recipe card directions for serving and storing.

CHRISTMAS ESSENCE

1 stick cinnamon
5 whole cloves
½ teaspoon nutmeg
½ teaspoon oil of cloves
½ teaspoon oil of cinnamon

Mix spices together and put in a small bag made from Christmas-patterned fabric. Add a card with directions for use: Mix with 4 cups water and simmer on stove for fragrant aroma.

Gift Container: Tie the bag of Christmas essence to a colorful new tea kettle or heat-proof potpourri dish.

ORANGE-CINNAMON POTPOURRI

6 oranges
Whole cloves
2 ounces orange oil
6 drops cinnamon oil
10 cinnamon sticks

With potato peeler, peel long strips of peel, about ½-inch wide, from oranges. Stud peel with cloves. Pour orange and cinnamon oils over peel and cinnamon sticks; mix till well coated.

Gift Container: Pour potpourri in a pretty crystal dish and cover with cellophane or plastic wrap.

NO-BAKE MINI FRUIT CAKES

1 pound crushed graham crackers
8 cups mixed dried fruits (raisins,
  dates, peaches, pears, or apricots)
8 cups mixed unsalted nuts
  (almonds, pecans, walnuts, brazil
  nuts, or hazel nuts)
1 pound marshmallows
¾ cup evaporated milk

Mix the graham cracker crumbs, fruits, and nuts in large mixing bowl. In saucepan over medium heat, melt marshmallows with evaporated milk. Pour this mixture over fruits and nuts. Mix well. Prepare 15 mini loaf pans (3½x6 inches) by greasing lightly with margarine or butter. With hands moistened with water, pack mixture tightly into pans. Garnish tops with a pecan half or piece of dried fruit. Cover and refrigerate for 12 to 24 hours. Remove cakes from pans; wrap in plastic wrap. Store in refrigerator or freezer. Tie with bow for Christmas giving.

PEANUTTY-CHOCO JUMBLE

6 ounces milk chocolate chips
6 ounces semisweet chocolate chips
1 cup peanut butter
1 box (12.3 ounces) Crispix cereal
2 cups powdered sugar

Melt chocolate chips and peanut butter in microwave or in double boiler over hot, not boiling, water. Pour mixture over cereal. Mix well. Pour powdered sugar in large brown paper bag. Add cereal mixture and shake till coated.

Gift Container: Pour into snack basket lined with plastic wrap, and decorate with ribbon.

PIONEER BEAN SOUP MIX

1 cup pinto beans
1 cup black beans
1 cup kidney beans
1 cup yellow split peas
1 cup black-eyed peas
1 cup lentils
1 cup green split peas
1 cup Great Northern beans

In clean pint jar, spoon 2 tablespoons of pinto beans in bottom; continue adding 2 tablespoons of each bean or pea variety in the order given till jar is full. Makes 4 pint jars. Screw on lid; cover with circle of gingham and tie with brown twine. Put the following recipe on a recipe card to enclose with the gift:

PIONEER BEAN SOUP

1 pint bean soup mix
7 cups water
1 ham hock
1 clove garlic, minced

1 large onion, chopped
1 teaspoon chili powder
1 to 2 teaspoons salt
1 8-ounce can tomato
  sauce
2 carrots, chopped
1 rib celery, chopped

Place all ingredients in a slow-cooker pot. Cover and cook on medium for 7 hours or till beans are tender. Or place in stock pot and cook on stove at simmer. Remove meat from ham hock and return to soup. Before serving, add juice of one lemon and top soup with grated cheese or sour cream. Makes 6 to 8 servings.

CHILI CON QUESO

2 pounds processed American cheese
2 12-ounce cans evaporated milk
2 4-ounce cans chopped green chilies

Cut cheese into chunks and place in glass bowl. Add milk and chilies. Microcook till cheese is melted, stirring 2 or 3 times. Or heat in top of double boiler till cheese is melted. Pour into clean glass jars. Makes about 4 pints. Store in refrigerator.

Gift Container: Attach to each jar a bow and gift card with directions for use as a vegetable dip, spread for crackers, heated sauce for vegetables, or sauce to pour over nachos.

PEANUT BUTTER DELIGHTS

1 20-ounce roll peanut butter cookie
dough
48 miniature peanut butter cup
candy bars

Preheat oven to 350 degrees F. Slice dough into ¾-inch slices. Cut each slice into quarters. Place each quarter in ungreased cup of mini-muffin pan. Bake for 8 to 10 minutes. Remove from oven and immediately press a peanut butter cup gently and evenly into each cookie. Cool before removing from pan. Refrigerate till chocolate is firm. Makes 48 cookies.

Gift Container: Put cookies on holiday gift platters or candy dishes and cover with plastic wrap. Place a bright Christmas bow on top of each gift.

PUMPKIN CAKE ROLL

3 eggs
1 cup sugar
⅔ cup canned or cooked pumpkin
1 teaspoon lemon juice
¾ cup flour
1 teaspoon baking powder
2 teaspoons cinnamon
1 teaspoon ginger
½ teaspoon nutmeg
½ teaspoon salt
½ cup chopped nuts
Powdered sugar

FILLING
2 3-ounce packages cream cheese,
  softened
¼ cup soft margarine
1 cup powdered sugar
½ teaspoon vanilla

Preheat oven to 350 degrees F. Beat eggs till lemon colored. Gradually add sugar. Stir in pumpkin and lemon juice. Sift flour, baking powder, cinnamon, ginger, nutmeg, and salt; add to egg-pumpkin mixture. Line a 10x15-inch jelly-roll pan with wax paper, and grease paper. Pour batter into pan; sprinkle with chopped nuts. Bake for 15 minutes. Sprinkle powdered sugar on kitchen towel. Turn cake onto towel, and remove wax paper. Roll up cake and towel lengthwise. Cool. Refrigerate or freeze.

Prepare Filling: Whip cream cheese and margarine. Beat in 1 cup powdered sugar and vanilla. Unroll cake and spread with filling. Roll up again. Cut in half. Wrap each roll in plastic wrap.

COCO-DATE BALLS

1 cup chopped dates
¾ cup sugar
2 eggs
1 teaspoon vanilla
2 cups flaked coconut
1 cup chopped nuts
1 cup rice cereal
1 cup corn-flake cereal

Mix dates, sugar, and eggs in heavy saucepan. Stir over medium heat till mixture is thick and leaves sides of pan, about 10 minutes. Remove from heat and cool slightly. Add remaining ingredients and stir till well mixed.

Wet hands and roll mixture into 1-inch balls. Roll in additional coconut. Makes 32 balls.

Gift container: Place balls in plastic storage container with lid. Tie with Christmas ribbon.

BETTY'S MOLDED MINTS

1 8-ounce package cream cheese,
* room temperature*
2 pounds powdered sugar, sifted
Peppermint flavoring
Food colorings

In mixer, whip cream cheese till fluffy. Gradually add powdered sugar. Knead like pie dough when too heavy for mixer; knead in flavoring and coloring. Roll into small balls. Sprinkle holiday candy molds with granulated sugar. Firmly press ball into candy mold; then unmold onto wax paper. Let candy set for 2 hours; then store in covered container or freeze.

Gift container: Place in small enameled tins with lids or crystal cream-and-sugar set.

LAYERED CHRISTMAS JELLY

*3 quarts bottled, canned, or
  reconstituted frozen apple juice
Food coloring and flavorings (see
  below)
3 boxes powdered pectin
15 cups sugar*

For each layer (see below) combine 1 quart juice, food coloring, flavoring, and 1 box pectin in heavy saucepan and bring to full boil. Add 5 cups sugar and bring to boil again. Boil 2 minutes. Remove from heat; skim. Pour into hot, sterilized jars about ⅓ full. Let set 2 hours. Repeat with colors and flavors. When last layer is set, pour thin layer of paraffin on top. Cover with lids. Makes 6 pints.

Minted Apple: Add about 5 drops green food color and 1½ teaspoons peppermint extract to apple juice.

Cinnamon Apple: Add ⅓ cup red cinnamon candies to apple juice.

Lemon Apple: Add juice of 2 lemons to apple juice.

RED PEPPER JELLY

About 7 large red bell peppers
2 cups cider vinegar
2 teaspoons salt
2 teaspoons chili powder
10 cups sugar
⅔ cup fresh or bottled lemon juice
1 6-ounce bottle liquid pectin

Cut peppers in chunks. Chop in blender or food processor to make 4 cups. Mix peppers, vinegar, salt, and chili powder in large pan and boil 10 minutes, stirring occasionally. Add sugar and lemon juice and bring back to a boil. Add pectin and boil 1 minute. Skim foam. Remove from heat and pour into sterilized jars and seal. Makes 10 to 12 half-pints. Serve with cream cheese as spread for assorted crackers or accompaniment to meat.

TUTTI–FRUITI PEAR JAM

3 cups fresh pears, chopped or
*   ground (about 2 pounds)*
1½ cups crushed pineapple with juice
1 6-ounce jar chopped maraschino
*   cherries, drained*
¼ cup lemon juice
1 package powdered pectin
5 cups sugar

Mix pears, pineapple, cherries, lemon juice, and pectin in heavy saucepan and bring to hard boil. Add sugar and bring to boil again. Boil 1 minute. Pour into sterilized jars and seal. Makes 8 half-pints.

LEMON CURD

⅔ cup lemon juice (about 4 fresh
  lemons)
4 teaspoons grated lemon peel
5 eggs
1 cup sugar
½ cup melted butter

Combine lemon juice and peel, eggs, and sugar; beat till smooth. Gradually add melted butter. Transfer mixture to small saucepan and cook over medium heat, stirring constantly, for 5 minutes, or till thickened. Pour into sterilized jars and seal, or cover and refrigerate or freeze. Lemon Curd keeps in refrigerator for 1 week or in freezer for several months. Makes about 3 half-pints. Serve as spread for hot scones, biscuits, toast, or other breads. Lemon Curd may also be used as filling for cake.

CRANBERRY CONSERVE

2 cups water
2 cups brown sugar
2 12-ounce packages fresh cranberries
4 oranges, peeled and chopped
1 tablespoon grated orange rind
2 apples, pared and chopped
1 cup chopped nuts

Mix water and brown sugar in heavy saucepan; bring to boil. Stir in cranberries, chopped oranges, orange rind, and chopped apples. Cook rapidly for 20 minutes. Stir in nuts. Pour into sterilized jars. Cover tightly and cool. Refrigerate or freeze no longer than 3 months. Makes 5 half-pint jars. Serve as accompaniment to poultry or as spread for toast, crackers, or bread.

BASIC FRUIT JAM OR TOPPING

2 cups mashed fruit
2 cups water
1 package unsweetened punch
    powder
1 package powdered pectin
Juice of 1 lemon
6 cups sugar

Mix fruit, water, punch powder, pectin, and lemon juice in saucepan. Bring to boil; add sugar and boil 3 minutes. Remove from heat; skim. Pour into sterilized jars; seal and cool.

Variations: Use strawberries with strawberry punch powder; raspberries with raspberry punch powder; peaches with orange punch powder, and so forth. This jam is slightly thin and makes excellent ice cream topping or syrup for pancakes or waffles.

ZUCCHINI PRESERVES

2 cups pared, grated zucchini
⅓ cup lemon juice
2 tablespoons grated lemon rind
1 box powdered pectin
4 cups sugar

Mix zucchini, lemon juice, lemon rind, and pectin in heavy saucepan. Bring to boil. Add sugar and bring to boil again; boil 2 minutes, stirring constantly. Take off heat and stir 5 minutes. Ladle into sterilized pint jars and screw on lids. Process in hot water bath or steam canner for 10 minutes. Serve as spread for toast, crackers, or breads.

SWEET-DILL CHIPS

1 46-ounce jar Kosher baby dill pickles
3 cups sugar
2 large cloves garlic, sliced
1 cup cider vinegar
10 whole cloves
1 3-inch cinnamon stick

Drain pickles and discard liquid. Cut into chunks and pack back into same jar or into 2 or 3 smaller jars. Combine sugar, garlic, vinegar, and spices in saucepan and bring to boil; simmer 5 minutes. Pour sauce over pickles; cool. Cover jars with lids and refrigerate. Flavor improves after 5 days.

CHILI SAUCE

40 large tomatoes
4 large onions, ground
4 green peppers, ground
1 tablespoon allspice
1 tablespoon cloves
1 tablespoon cinnamon
1 tablespoon nutmeg
2 tablespoons salt
3 cups vinegar
2 cups sugar

Scald, peel, and quarter tomatoes. Place in large kettle and add remaining ingredients. Simmer for 2 to 3 hours till desired thickness, stirring often to keep from scorching. Pour into jars; screw on lids and process in hot water bath or steam canner for 10 minutes. Makes 8 to 10 pints.

WATERMELON PICKLES

3 quarts watermelon rind (about 6
  pounds rind, unpared)
¾ cup salt
3 quarts water
2 quarts crushed ice
8 cups sugar
3 cups white vinegar
3 cups water
1 tablespoon whole cloves
3 cinnamon sticks
1 lemon, thinly sliced
Red or green food coloring

Pare green skin from watermelon rind. Cut rind into 1-inch cubes. Make brine by mixing salt and 3 quarts water; add crushed ice. Pour brine over watermelon and let stand 5 to 6 hours. Drain, then rinse in cold water. Cover with cold water and bring to boil; cook 10 minutes. Drain. Combine sugar, vinegar, 3 cups water, cloves, and cinnamon sticks. Boil 5 minutes, then pour over watermelon. Add lemon slices and few drops of food coloring. Let pickles stand overnight. Reheat and cook about 10 minutes. Pour into jars; screw on lids and process in hot water bath or steam canner for 10 minutes. Makes 4 to 5 pints.

PICKLED BEETS

3 quarts cooked and peeled small
  beets
1½ cups water
2 cups sugar
3½ cups cider vinegar
1 tablespoon whole allspice
2 sticks cinnamon
1 teaspoon salt

To cook fresh beets, cut tops off, leaving 2 inches of stems and the tap roots. Wash and cover with water. Boil till tender. Drain and cool. Slip skins off. Set aside. Combine remaining ingredients and simmer 15 minutes. Pack beets into jars; pour hot syrup over beets, leaving ½-inch head space; screw on lids. Process 25 minutes in hot water bath or steam canner. Makes about 6 pints.

BREAD AND BUTTER PICKLES

2 gallons (16 cups) sliced cucumbers
14 small white onions, sliced
4 large green peppers, chopped
1 large red pepper, chopped
¾ cup salt
Water
8 cups sugar
1 tablespoon turmeric
1 teaspoon cloves
1 teaspoon celery seed
¼ cup mustard seed
2½ quarts cider vinegar

Slice cucumbers ⅛-inch thick. Place in 6-quart pan and stir in onions and peppers. Sprinkle with salt. Cover with cold water, cover, and let stand for 3 hours. Drain. Make syrup by combining sugar, turmeric, cloves, celery seed, mustard seed, and vinegar in saucepan. Heat till sugar is dissolved. Pour syrup over cucumber mixture and bring to boil. Pack in pint canning jars; screw on lids. Process in hot water bath or steam canner for 15 minutes to seal. Makes 16 pints.

INDEX